Bread Machine Cookbook

Quick and Easy Bread Machine Recipes

Louise Davidson

Copyrights

All rights reserved © 2018 by Louise Davidson and The cookbook Publisher. No part of this publication or the information in it may be quoted from or reproduced in any form by means such as printing, scanning, photocopying, or otherwise without prior written permission of the copyright holder.

Disclaimer and Terms of Use

Effort has been made to ensure that the information in this book is accurate and complete. However, the author and the publisher do not warrant the accuracy of the information, text, and graphics contained within the book due to the rapidly changing nature of science, research, known and unknown facts, and internet. The author and the publisher do not hold any responsibility for errors, omissions, or contrary interpretation of the subject matter herein.

The recipes provided in this book are for informational purposes only and are not intended to provide dietary advice. A medical practitioner should be consulted before making any changes in diet. Additionally, recipe cooking times may require adjustment depending on age and quality of appliances. Readers are strongly urged to take all precautions to ensure ingredients are fully cooked to avoid the dangers of foodborne illnesses. The nutritional information for recipes contained in this book are provided for informational purposes only. This information is based on the specific brands, ingredients, and measurements used to make the recipe and therefore the nutritional information is an estimate, and in no way is intended to be a guarantee of the actual nutritional value of the recipe made in the reader's home. The author and the publisher will not be responsible for any damages resulting in your reliance on the nutritional information. The best method to obtain an accurate count of the nutritional value in the recipe is to calculate the information with your specific brands, ingredients, and measurements. The recipes and suggestions provided in this book are solely the opinion of the author. The author and publisher do not take any responsibility for any consequences that may result due to following the instructions provided in this book.

ISBN: 9781730927812

Printed in the United States

Contents

Introduction _____ 1

Getting to Know Your Bread Machine _____ 5

and Baking Techniques _____ 5

Everyday & Multigrain Breads _____ 19

Gluten Free Breads _____ 67

Fruit Breads _____ 91

Spice and Nut Breads _____ 115

Vegetable Breads _____ 133

Cheese and Herb Breads _____ 149

Sweet Breads _____ 171

Specialty and Holiday Breads _____ 201

Recipe Index _____ 231

Conversion Tables _____ 237

INTRODUCTION

The aroma of freshly baked bread is simply magical, and the crispy crust is simply irresistible. The culinary world would be woefully incomplete without breads in it. A slice of bread with breakfast makes our morning perfect, two slices for lunch makes a sandwich, and a slice for dinner complements all manner of delicious meals and soups.

Unfortunately, traditional bread making demands hours of time and years of experience to create dough that will rise and bake as it should. In the modern era, we hardly have enough time to complete day-to-day tasks, let alone several spare hours for baking bread. That's where bread machines come in.

A bread maker or bread machine is a convenient kitchen appliance that simplifies the complex task of bread making. Absolutely no baking experience is required to make bread with a bread machine; it is as simple as it looks. A bread machine does all the work for you, including mixing, kneading, rising and baking. You just put the ingredients into it. You don't have to go through the tedious process of kneading dough and waiting for it to rise.

A bread machine comes with a bread pan, mixing paddles, and a heating element to create warmth that will help the bread rise. It has many pre-set functions to bake a wide variety of breads, including basic breads, wholegrain breads, sweet breads, fruit breads and so on.

This exclusive cookbook on bread machines provides thorough guidance on the different aspects of preparing breads effortlessly at home. It includes detailed sections covering:

- Basic bread ingredients
- Different bread machine cycles/settings
- Advantages of bread machines
- The right order for adding ingredients to a bread machine
- The role of gluten
- Ideal ways to store your breads
- Tips for baking perfectly textured breads
- Troubleshooting

This expansive book includes a range of bread recipes to prepare using your all-time favorite spices, fruits, nuts, vegetables, and cheese. Explore the secrets of baking homemade Basic Breads, Sweet Breads, Fruit/Nut Breads, Spice Breads, Vegetables Breads, Holiday Breads, Gluten-Free Breads, Sourdough Breads, Specialty Breads, Cheese Breads, and Spice/Nut Breads. All the recipes are easy to follow and suitable for both bread machine beginners and experts.

Make your weekends with your friends and family special by serving them freshly baked homemade breads. Get ready to learn the secrets of baking foolproof loaves at home with an amazing bread machine. Let's get started!

Advantage of Bread Machines

Owning a bread machine is a great advantage for your busy lifestyle as it not only saves time in the kitchen but also makes your life better in many ways.

Fresh Bread Anytime
Traditional oven baking is not so much a single task as a series of steps. It requires careful planning to get baked bread out of your oven. Of course you can purchase bread from your local bakery, but it's not always freshly baked. With a bread machine, you do not have to plan in advance as all you need to do is add the ingredients and start the machine. You can enjoy freshly baked bread anytime you want it.

Ingredient Freedom
You don't have any choice as to the ingredients in commercially available breads. With a bread machine, you can customize the taste and texture of your breads because you have the freedom to add your favorite fruits, spices, herbs, cheese and so on and enjoy your choice of flavors.

Effortless and Clutterless
Traditional bread making makes lots of mess what with all the mixing and kneading. A bread machine creates no mess at all, as everything from mixing to baking is done within the bread pan.

Healthy & Economical
When you add up the cost of store-bought bread over the years, a bread machine is a much more economical choice. More importantly, it is a smart way to enjoy freshly baked bread with healthy ingredients as you can choose the flour and everything else that goes into it.

Getting to Know Your Bread Machine and Baking Techniques

Before learning to make aromatic, delicious breads, you need to understand the basics of bread baking and the basic functions of a bread machine. Bread machines are also popularly known as bread makers. They function in a very systemic way and go though many steps to complete the baking process.

Bread Machine Cycles/Settings

Bread machines offer many different settings for baking different varieties of breads such as gluten-free, whole wheat bread, basic white bread, sweet bread etc. After you add ingredients to the bread machine and start the baking process, the mixture goes through many cycles before coming out as a perfectly textured bread.

Basic/White
Use this setting for all basic breads, including white breads and many other breads. The commonly used flour for this setting is white bread flour, and the average duration is 3–4 hours.

Wholegrain/Whole Wheat
Given their heavy, high-gluten texture, whole wheat and wholegrain flours need longer kneading and rising times. Use this setting to prepare all types of wholegrain and whole wheat breads.

Gluten-Free
This setting is suitable for preparing all types of gluten-free breads using flour other than wheat flour. A gluten-free diet is becoming a popular choice for millions of health-conscious people across the world. However, there still aren't that many commercial gluten-free breads available, and those that exist tend to be a little expensive. One great advantage of a bread machine is that you can prepare all types of gluten-free breads with your choice of ingredients to suit your taste and texture preferences as well as your budget.

Quick/Rapid
Use this setting for breads with lower rising times and overall shorter baking times. Generally speaking this means breads with no yeast requirement, which require less baking time than other breads; however, this setting is also appropriate for some breads with yeast. Time varies from 30 minutes to 2 hours.

Dough
This setting is for preparing dough without baking the bread. It's quite useful when you're planning to bake in the oven but want to skip the kneading part. One advantage of this setting is that baking in the oven lets you create breads of different shapes. After you add the required ingredients, the bread machine mixes them and kneads a flaky dough for you. Most machines knead the dough till first rise.

Fruit/Nut
Use this setting for preparing breads with added fruits and nuts. Many machines have a fruit/nut hopper to grind the added ingredients while the kneading process is going on. The machine will either add the nuts/fruits automatically during the baking process or signal when the time is right for you to do it.

Sweet
Use this setting for breads with a high amount of sweet and/or fatty ingredients, as well as for breads prepared from cheese and/or eggs. Sweet breads require less baking time and lower baking temperature to avoid an overly dark crust.

French
Use this setting for breads that need little or no sugar. French breads need higher temperatures and longer rising times, and they typically have hard crusts.

Jam
Some bread makers are equipped with a jam setting to make jam your own jams. What goes better with warm breads than jam and butter? The manufacturer will usually include recipes for this setting as it is beyond the scope of this cookbook.

Timed-Bake
This setting is like a timer for your bread machine: You add all the ingredients and the machine processes them later. For example, you can add the ingredients right before leaving for work and set the timer for mid-afternoon. The machine will start baking at the set time, and you can enjoy freshly baked bread when you return home. As the ingredients will stay inside the bread pan for a while, it is not recommended to use this setting for recipes that include perishable ingredients such as milk, cream, cheese and eggs.

Steps in Making Bread

Bread machines have made the complex task of bread making as simple as possible. You do not need to master the skill of kneading the dough or worry about dough rise or baking consistency. In a few easy steps, you can make many different varieties of breads with automatic bread machine functions.

Measure Ingredients
The first step involves measuring the ingredients specified in a recipe. Measure them as per your preferred bread size. The most popular bread sizes are 1½ pounds (12 slices) and 2 pounds (16 slices), although 1-pound and 2½-pound sizes are also used.
The recipes in this book include ingredient measurements for 1½-pound and 2-pound loaves. If you want to make a 1-pound or 2½-pound loaf, you will have to adjust your ingredient quantities accordingly. You can look at the conversion table at the end of the book for easy adjustments.

For 1½-pound and 2-pound breads, the bread pan capacity should be at least 10 cups and 12 cups respectively.

Bread Pan
After measuring the ingredients, take out the bread pan provided by the manufacturer. Add the ingredients to the pan in the order specified in the recipe. Yeast is added last to keep it separate from liquid ingredients for better fermentation.

A standard order for adding ingredients, which will give the best results for most recipes, is:

1. Wet Ingredients
2. Dry Ingredients
3. Yeast

The order of ingredients is covered in more detail in the following section.

Select Function
Follow the recipe instructions to select the appropriate function from the available options (Basic/White, Wholegrain, Sweet, etc.).

Select Loaf Size
After selecting a function, select the loaf size (1, 1½, 2, or 2½ pounds) based on the ingredient measurements.

Select Crust Type
Most bread machines have three choices for preparing breads with different crust types:

- Light
- Medium
- Dark

After selecting the crust type, start the machine and it will start mixing the dough and baking the bread.

Cooling & Slicing
Take out the bread pan after the machine signals the end of the baking process. Allow it to cool down for 5–10 minutes, then shake the bread pan to loosen the bread, take out the loaf, slice and serve.

Bread Baking Steps

Just like you would if you were baking bread the old-fashioned way, a bread machine goes through multiple steps before giving you a fresh loaf.

1. The first step is combining the ingredients in the bread pan. This is followed by a brief resting period.
2. The bread machine kneads the mixture thorough its paddles to create gluten strands. Different machines knead for different amounts of time, but usually this step takes 20–30 minutes.
3. Yeast facilitates the fermentation process during which a kneaded dough goes through its first rise. By metabolizing sugar or other sweeteners, the yeast extends the gluten strands to inflate the dough.
4. After the first rise come the second and third rises. This usually doubles the size of the dough. Depending on the ingredients, the first rise takes place from 5–40 minutes after the ingredients are added.
5. After the rising is complete, the bread machine starts its heating element to begin the baking process. Different bread machines have different baking times; the duration also depends on the loaf size and crust setting used. After the end of the baking process, your loaf is ready to slice and serve.

Basic Bread Ingredients and Order of Addition

Breads consist of a few very basic ingredients flour, liquids, yeast, butter, etc. Knowing the role of these ingredients helps you to understand the baking process. Moreover, the order in which you add ingredients is crucial when making breads in your bread machine. Do not commit the cardinal sin of bread making by adding the ingredients randomly to the bread pan.
The following sections highlight the correct order to put ingredients in the bread pan to bake perfect breads.

Water/Milk
All of the other basic bread ingredients, including flour, salt and yeast, need a liquid medium to do their respective tasks. Water is the most common liquid ingredient; milk, buttermilk, cream and juice are some common substitutes.

The liquid is usually the first ingredient to be added to the bread pan. This is very important as it maintains the ideal texture of your bread. The liquid should not be cold; ensure that it is lukewarm (between 80 and 90°F) whenever possible.

Butter/Oil
Butter, oil or fat is usually added after the liquid. This is what gives bread crust its attractive brown color and crispy texture. Do not use cold butter that has just been taken out of the refrigerator. You can either microwave it for a few seconds or keep it at room temperature until it gets soft.

Sugar/honey (if using)
Sweet ingredients such as honey, corn syrup, maple syrup and sugar are usually added after the butter as they mix easily with water and butter. However, the sweetener can be added before

the butter as well. Sugar, honey, etc. serve as a feeding medium for yeast, so fermentation is stronger with the addition of sweet ingredients.

Eggs (if using)
Eggs need to be at room temperature before they are added to the bread pan. If the eggs are taken from the refrigerator, keep them outside at room temperature until they are no longer cold. They keep the crust tender and add protein and flavor to the bread.

Chilled Ingredients
If you are using any other ingredient that is kept chilled, such as cheese, milk, buttermilk or cream, keep it outside at room temperature until it is no longer cold, or microwave it for a few seconds to warm it up.

Salt
Use table salt or non-iodized salt for better results. Salt that is high in iodine can hamper the activity of the yeast and create problems with fermentation. Furthermore, salt itself is a yeast inhibitor and should not be touching yeast directly; that is why salt and yeast are never added together or one after another.

Spices (if using)
Spices such as cinnamon, nutmeg and ginger are often used to add flavor to breads. They may be added before or after the flour.

Flour
Flour is the primary ingredient for any bread recipe. It contains gluten (except for the gluten-free flours) and protein, and when the yeast produces alcohol and carbon dioxide, the gluten and protein trap the alcohol and carbon dioxide to initiate the bread making process.

There are many different types of flours used for preparing different types of breads. Bread machine flour or white bread flour is the most common type as it is suitable for most bread recipes. It's so versatile because it contains an ideal proportion of protein for bread baking.

Usually flour is stored at room temperature, but if you keep your flour in your fridge, allow it to warm up before using it.

Seeds (if using)
If a recipe calls for adding seeds such as sunflower seeds or caraway seeds, these should be added after the flour. However, when there are two different flours being used, it is best to add the seeds in between the flours for a better mix.

Yeast
Yeast is the ingredient responsible for initiating the vital bread making process of fermentation. Yeast needs the right amount of heat, moisture and liquid to grow and multiply. When yeast multiplies, it releases alcohol and carbon dioxide.

You can use active dry yeast or bread machine yeast (both will be available in local grocery stores). Cool, dry places are ideal to store yeast packs.

Yeast is added to the bread pan last, after the flour and other dry ingredients. (For certain breads, like fruit/nut bread, yeast is technically not the last ingredient, as the fruits or nuts are added later by the machine. However, yeast is the last ingredient to be added before starting the bread machine.)

Tips for Making Perfect Breads

When you are using a bread machine for the first time, it's common to have some concerns. However, they are quite easy to fix. The following are some useful tips and quick-and-easy fixes for the most common problems encountered while baking bread in a bread machine.

Dough Check
You can check the progress of the dough while the bread machine is mixing the ingredients. Take a quick check after 5 minutes of kneading. An ideal dough with the right amount of dry and wet ingredients makes one smooth ball and feels slightly tacky. You can open the lid to evaluate the dough. Do not worry about interfering with the kneading process by opening the lid; the bread structure won't be affected even if you poke it to get a feel for the dough.

If the dough feels too wet/moist or does not form into a ball shape, you can add 1 tablespoon of flour at a time and check again after a few minutes. If you feel that the dough is too dry, or it has formed two or three small balls, you can add 1 teaspoon of water at a time and check again after a few minutes.

Fruit/Nut Bread
When making fruit or nut breads, it is very important to add the fruits or nuts at the right time. Not all bread machines come with a nut/fruit dispenser or hopper. If yours doesn't have one, don't worry; the machine will signal you with a beep series when it's time to add the fruits or nuts.

Citrus Ingredients

Citrus ingredients such as lemon zest, orange zest, orange juice, lemon juice and pineapple juice can create issues with yeast fermentation if added in excess. Do not add more than the quantity specified in a recipe. The same goes for alcohol and cinnamon.

Salt Adjustment

When making small loaves (around 1 pound), sometimes the loaf rises more or less than expected. In many such instances, the issue is with the quantity of salt added. To avoid problems, try using less salt or cutting back on the quantity specified in the recipe. Using sea salt or coarse salt can also help prevent problems with small loaves.

Bread Collapse

The amount of yeast is very important for proper rising. The most common reason for bread collapse during the baking process is adding too much or too little yeast. Do not add more yeast than specified in the recipe. Also check the expiration date on the yeast pack; freshly packed yeast provides the best results. Other reasons for bread collapse are using cold water and adding excess salt.

Failure to Rise

Many factors can contribute to the failure of a dough to rise completely. Insufficient gluten content, miscalculated ingredients, excess salt, excess sugar, and using cold ingredients are the most common reasons. Always warm any chilled ingredients or place them at room temperature for a while before adding them to the bread pan. However, if you are warming any ingredients in your oven, make sure not to overheat them. They need to be lukewarm, at between 80 and 90°F, and not too hot. Also make sure that the yeast does not come in direct contact with the salt, as this creates problems with rising (that is why yeast is added last).

Texture Troubles

- If your bread has a coarse texture, try adding more salt and reducing the amount of liquid.
- If your bread looks small and feels dense, try using flour with a higher protein content. Bread flour has a sufficient amount of protein, but slightly denser loaves are common when you use heavier flours such as rye flour and whole wheat flour. Use additional ingredients such as fruits, nuts and vegetables in their specified quantities. Adding too much of such ingredients will make your loaf too heavy, small and dense.
- Moist or gummy loaves are less common, but it can happen if you have added too much liquid or used too much sugar. Too much liquid can also result in a doughy center.
- If you bread has an unbrowned top, try adding more sugar. This can also happen if your bread machine has a glass top.
- If your loaf has a mushroom top, it is probably due to too much yeast or water. Try reducing the amount of water and/or yeast.
- Sometimes a baked loaf has some flour on one side. When you bake the next time, try scrapping off any visible flour during the kneading cycle with a rubber spatula.
- If your loaf has an overly dark crust, try using the Medium crust setting next time. This also happens if you've added too much sugar and when you fail to take out the bread pan after the end of the baking process. It is always advisable to remove the bread pan right after the process is complete.

- If your loaf has a sunken top, it is probably because of using too much liquid or overly hot ingredients. This is also common during humid or warm weather.

Excess Rise

Many times a loaf rises more than expected; the most common reasons are too much yeast, too little salt and using cold water. But also make sure that the capacity of your bread pan is sufficient for the size of loaf you have selected; trying to make a large loaf in a small bread pan will obviously lead to such trouble.

Paddles

After the bread machine completes its baking process the paddles may remain inside the bread loaf. Allow the freshly made bread to cool down and then place it on a cutting board and gently take out the paddles.

Spraying the paddles with a cooking spray before you add the ingredients to the bread pan will make it easier to clean them after the bread is baked.

Cleaning

After you take the baked loaf from the bread pan, do not immerse the pan in water. Rather, fill it with warm soapy water.

Note: for the recipe containing eggs, please assume that we use large eggs unless specified otherwise.

EVERYDAY & MULTIGRAIN BREADS

Classic White Bread I

Makes 1 loaf

Ingredients

<u>16 slice bread (2 pounds)</u>
1½ cups lukewarm water
1 tablespoon + 1 teaspoon olive oil
1½ teaspoons sugar
1 teaspoon table salt
¼ teaspoon baking soda
2½ cups all-purpose flour
1 cup white bread flour
2½ teaspoons bread machine yeast

<u>12 slice bread (1½ pounds)</u>
1⅛ cups lukewarm water
¾ tablespoon + 1 teaspoon olive oil
1⅛ teaspoons sugar
¾ teaspoon table salt
⅛ teaspoon baking soda
1½ cups all-purpose flour
¾ cup white bread flour
1½ teaspoons bread machine yeast

Directions
1. Choose the size of loaf you would like to make and measure your ingredients.
2. Add the ingredients to the bread pan in the order listed above.
3. Place the pan in the bread machine and close the lid.

4. Turn on the bread maker. Select the White/Basic setting, then the loaf size, and finally the crust color. Start the cycle.
5. When the cycle is finished and the bread is baked, carefully remove the pan from the machine. Use a pot holder as the handle will be very hot. Let rest for a few minutes.
6. Remove the bread from the pan and allow to cool on a wire rack for at least 10 minutes before slicing.

Nutrition per slice
Calories 124, fat 4.9 g, carbs 17.2 g, sodium 178 mg, protein 2 g

Classic White Bread II

Makes 1 loaf

Ingredients

<u>16 slice bread (2 pounds)</u>
1 1/2 cups water, lukewarm between 80 and 90°F
3 tablespoons unsalted butter, melted
1 tablespoon sugar
3 tablespoons dry milk powder
1 1/4 teaspoons table salt
4 cup white bread flour
1 1/2 teaspoons bread machine yeast

<u>12 slice bread (1 ½ pounds)</u>
1 1/4 cups water, lukewarm between 80 and 90°F
2 tablespoons unsalted butter, melted
2 teaspoons sugar
2 tablespoons dry milk powder
1 teaspoons table salt
3 1/4 cup white bread flour
1 1/4 teaspoons bread machine yeast

Directions

1. Choose the size of loaf you would like to make and measure your ingredients.
2. Add the ingredients to the bread pan in the order listed above.
3. Place the pan in the bread machine and close the lid.
4. Turn on the bread maker. Select the White/Basic setting, then the loaf size, and finally the crust color. Start the cycle.

5. When the cycle is finished and the bread is baked, carefully remove the pan from the machine. Use a pot holder as the handle will be very hot. Let rest for a few minutes.
6. Remove the bread from the pan and allow to cool on a wire rack for at least 10 minutes before slicing.

Nutrition per slice
Calories 148, fat 3.6 g, carbs 23.4 g,
sodium 197 mg, protein 3.4 g

Classic White Sandwich Bread

Makes 1 loaf

Ingredients

<u>16 slice bread (2 pounds)</u>
1 cup water, lukewarm between 80 and 90°F
2 tablespoons unsalted butter, melted
1 teaspoon table salt
1/4 cup sugar
2 egg whites or 1 egg, beaten
3 cups white bread flour
1 1/2 teaspoons bread machine yeast

<u>12 slice bread (1 ½ pounds)</u>
3/4 cup water, lukewarm between 80 and 90°F
1 1/2 tablespoons unsalted butter, melted
3/4 teaspoon table salt
1 ½ ounces sugar
2 egg whites or 1 egg, beaten
2 1/4 cups white bread flour
1 1/8 teaspoons bread machine yeast

Directions

1. Choose the size of loaf you would like to make and measure your ingredients.
2. Add the ingredients to the bread pan in the order listed above.
3. Place the pan in the bread machine and close the lid.
4. Turn on the bread maker. Select the White/Basic setting, then the loaf size, and finally the crust color. Start the cycle.

5. When the cycle is finished and the bread is baked, carefully remove the pan from the machine. Use a pot holder as the handle will be very hot. Let rest for a few minutes.
6. Remove the bread from the pan and allow to cool on a wire rack for at least 10 minutes before slicing.

Nutrition per slice
Calories 126, fat 2.3 g, carbs 23 g, sodium 137 mg, protein 4 g

Baguette Style French Bread

Makes 2 loaves

Ingredients

2 baguettes of 1-pound each
Ingredients for bread machine
1 ⅔ cups water, lukewarm between 80 and 90°F
1 teaspoon table salt
4 ⅔ cups white bread flour
2 ⅔ teaspoons bread machine yeast or rapid raise yeast

2 baguettes of ¾-pound each
Ingredients for bread machine
1 ¼ cups water, lukewarm between 80 and 90°F
¾ teaspoon table salt
3 ½ cups white bread flour
2 teaspoons bread machine yeast or rapid raise yeast

Other Ingredients
Corn meal
Olive oil
1 egg white
1 tablespoon water

Directions

1. Choose the size of crusty breads you would like to make and measure your ingredients.
2. Add the ingredients for the bread machine to the bread pan in the order listed above.
3. Place the pan in the bread machine and close the lid. Turn on the bread maker. Select the dough/manual setting.

4. When the dough cycle is completed, remove the pan and lay the dough on floured working surface.
5. Knead the dough a few times and add flour if needed so the dough is not too sticky to handle. Cut the dough in half and form a ball with each half.
6. Grease a baking sheet with olive oil. Dust lightly with corn meal.
7. Pre-heat the oven to 375^0 and place oven rack on the middle position.
8. With a rolling pin dusted with flour, roll one of the dough balls into a 12-inch by 9 -inch rectangle for the 2 pounds bread size or a 10-inch by 8-inch rectangle for the 1 ½ pound bread size. Starting on the longer side, roll the dough tightly. Pinch the ends and the seam with your fingers to seal. Roll the dough in a back in forth movement to make it into a nice French baguette shape.
9. Repeat the process with the second dough ball.
10. Place breads onto the baking sheet with the seams down and brush with some olive oil with enough space in between them to rise. Dust top of both loafs with a little bit of corn meal. Cover with a clean kitchen towel and place in a warm area with any air draught. Let rise for 10 to 15 minutes, or until it both breads have doubled in size.
11. Mix the egg white and 1 tablespoon of water and lightly brush over both breads.
12. Place in the oven and bake for 20 minutes. Remove from oven and brush with remaining egg wash on top of both breads. Place back into the oven taking care of turning around the baking sheet. Bake for another 5 to 10 minutes or until the baguettes are golden-brown. Let rest on a wired rack for 5-10 minutes before serving.

Nutrition per slice (about 32 g.)
Calories 87, fat 0.8 g, carbs 16.5 g, sodium 192 mg, protein 3.4 g

100% Whole Wheat Bread

Makes 1 loaf

Ingredients

<u>16 slice bread (2 pounds)</u>
1¼ cups lukewarm water
2 tablespoons vegetable oil or olive oil
¼ cup honey or maple syrup
1½ teaspoons table salt
3½ cups whole wheat flour
¼ cup sesame, sunflower, or flax seeds (optional)
1½ teaspoons bread machine yeast

<u>12 slice bread (1½ pounds)</u>
1 cup lukewarm water
1½ tablespoons vegetable oil or olive oil
3 tablespoons honey or maple syrup
1 teaspoon table salt
2⅔ cups whole wheat flour
3 tablespoons sesame, sunflower, or flax seeds (optional)
1 teaspoon bread machine yeast

Directions

1. Choose the size of loaf you would like to make and measure your ingredients.
2. Add the ingredients to the bread pan in the order listed above.
3. Place the pan in the bread machine and close the lid.
4. Turn on the bread maker. Select the Whole Wheat/Wholegrain setting, then the loaf size, and finally the crust color. Start the cycle.

5. When the cycle is finished, and the bread is baked, carefully remove the pan from the machine. Use a pot holder as the handle will be very hot. Let rest for a few minutes.
6. Remove the bread from the pan and allow to cool on a wire rack for at least 10 minutes before slicing.

Nutrition per slice
Calories 147, fat 5.8 g, carbs 22.1 g, sodium 138 mg, protein 3.4 g

Buttermilk Bread

Makes 1 loaf

Ingredients

<u>16 slice bread (2 pounds)</u>
1¼ cups lukewarm buttermilk
2 tablespoons unsalted butter, melted
2 tablespoons sugar
1½ teaspoons table salt
½ teaspoon baking powder
3½ cups white bread flour
2¼ teaspoons bread machine yeast

<u>12 slice bread (1½ pounds)</u>
1¼ cups lukewarm buttermilk
1½ tablespoons unsalted butter, melted
1½ tablespoons sugar
1⅛ teaspoons table salt
⅓ teaspoon baking powder
2⅔ cups white bread flour
1⅔ teaspoons bread machine yeast

Directions

1. Choose the size of loaf you would like to make and measure your ingredients.
2. Add the ingredients to the bread pan in the order listed above.
3. Place the pan in the bread machine and close the lid.
4. Turn on the bread maker. Select the White/Basic setting, then the loaf size, and finally the crust color. Start the cycle.

5. When the cycle is finished and the bread is baked, carefully remove the pan from the machine. Use a pot holder as the handle will be very hot. Let rest for a few minutes.
6. Remove the bread from the pan and allow to cool on a wire rack for at least 10 minutes before slicing.

Nutrition per slice
Calories 132, fat 2.2 g, carbs 23.4 g, sodium 234 mg, protein 4.3 g

Oat Molasses Bread

Makes 1 loaf

Ingredients

<u>16 slice bread (2 pounds)</u>
1⅓ cups boiling water
¾ cup old-fashioned oats
3 tablespoons butter
1 large egg, lightly beaten
2 teaspoons table salt
¼ cup honey
1½ tablespoons dark molasses
4 cups white bread flour
2½ teaspoons bread machine yeast

<u>12 slice bread (1½ pounds)</u>
1 cup boiling water
½ cup old-fashioned oats
2 tablespoons butter
1 large egg, lightly beaten
1½ teaspoons table salt
3 tablespoons honey
1 tablespoon dark molasses
3 cups white bread flour
2 teaspoons bread machine yeast

Directions

1. Add the boiling water and oats to a mixing bowl. Allow the oats to soak well and cool down completely. Do not drain the water.
2. Choose the size of loaf you would like to make and measure your ingredients.

3. Add the soaked oats, along with any remaining water, to the bread pan.
4. Add the remaining ingredients to the bread pan in the order listed above.
5. Place the pan in the bread machine and close the lid.
6. Turn on the bread maker. Select the White/Basic setting, then the loaf size, and finally the crust color. Start the cycle.
7. When the cycle is finished and the bread is baked, carefully remove the pan from the machine. Use a pot holder as the handle will be very hot. Let rest for a few minutes.
8. Remove the bread from the pan and allow to cool on a wire rack for at least 10 minutes before slicing.

Nutrition per slice
Calories 160, fat 7.1 g, carbs 18 g, sodium 164 mg, protein 5.1 g

Whole Wheat Corn Bread

Makes 1 loaf

Ingredients

<u>16 slice bread (2 pounds)</u>
1⅓ cups lukewarm water
2 tablespoons light brown sugar
1 large egg, beaten
2 tablespoons unsalted butter, melted
1½ teaspoons table salt
¾ cup whole wheat flour
¾ cup cornmeal
2¾ cups white bread flour
2½ teaspoons bread machine yeast

<u>12 slice bread (1½ pounds)</u>
1 cup lukewarm water
1½ tablespoons light brown sugar
1 medium egg, beaten
1½ tablespoons unsalted butter, melted
1½ teaspoons table salt
½ cup whole wheat flour
½ cup cornmeal
2 cups white bread flour
1½ teaspoons bread machine yeast

Directions

1. Choose the size of loaf you would like to make and measure your ingredients.
2. Add the ingredients to the bread pan in the order listed above.
3. Place the pan in the bread machine and close the lid.

4. Turn on the bread maker. Select the White/Basic setting, then the loaf size, and finally the crust color. Start the cycle.
5. When the cycle is finished and the bread is baked, carefully remove the pan from the machine. Use a pot holder as the handle will be very hot. Let rest for a few minutes.
6. Remove the bread from the pan and allow to cool on a wire rack for at least 10 minutes before slicing.

Nutrition per slice
Calories 146, fat 5.7 g, carbs 19.3 g,
sodium 124 mg, protein 4.8 g

Wheat Bran Bread

Makes 1 loaf

Ingredients

<u>16 slice bread (2 pounds)</u>
1½ cups lukewarm milk
3 tablespoons unsalted butter, melted
¼ cup sugar
2 teaspoons table salt
½ cup wheat bran
3½ cups white bread flour
2 teaspoons bread machine yeast

<u>12 slice bread (1½ pounds)</u>
1⅛ cups lukewarm milk
2¼ tablespoons unsalted butter, melted
3 tablespoons sugar
1½ teaspoons table salt
⅓ cup wheat bran
2⅔ cups white bread flour
1½ teaspoons bread machine yeast

Directions

1. Choose the size of loaf you would like to make and measure your ingredients.
2. Add the ingredients to the bread pan in the order listed above.
3. Place the pan in the bread machine and close the lid.
4. Turn on the bread maker. Select the White/Basic setting, then the loaf size, and finally the crust color. Start the cycle.

5. When the cycle is finished and the bread is baked, carefully remove the pan from the machine. Use a pot holder as the handle will be very hot. Let rest for a few minutes.
6. Remove the bread from the pan and allow to cool on a wire rack for at least 10 minutes before slicing.

Nutrition per slice
Calories 147, fat 2.8 g, carbs 24.6 g,
sodium 312 mg, protein 3.8 g

Rye Bread

Makes 1 loaf

Ingredients

<u>16 slice bread (2 pounds)</u>
1⅔ cups lukewarm water
¼ cup + 4 teaspoons Dijon mustard
2 tablespoons unsalted butter, melted
4 teaspoons sugar
1 teaspoon table salt
2 cups rye flour
2⅔ cups white bread flour
1½ teaspoons bread machine yeast

<u>12 slice bread (1½ pounds)</u>
1¼ cups lukewarm water
¼ cup Dijon mustard
1½ tablespoons unsalted butter, melted
1 tablespoon sugar
¾ teaspoon table salt
1½ cups rye flour
2 cups white bread flour
1 teaspoon bread machine yeast

Directions

1. Choose the size of loaf you would like to make and measure your ingredients.
2. Add the ingredients to the bread pan in the order listed above.
3. Place the pan in the bread machine and close the lid.
4. Turn on the bread maker. Select the White/Basic setting, then the loaf size, and finally the crust color. Start the cycle.

5. When the cycle is finished and the bread is baked, carefully remove the pan from the machine. Use a pot holder as the handle will be very hot. Let rest for a few minutes.
6. Remove the bread from the pan and allow to cool on a wire rack for at least 10 minutes before slicing.

Nutrition per slice
Calories 153, fat 2.1 g, carbs 24.8 g,
sodium 256 mg, protein 5.2 g

Classic Whole Wheat Bread

Makes 1 loaf

Ingredients

<u>16 slice bread (2 pounds)</u>
1 cup lukewarm water
½ cup unsalted butter, melted
2 eggs, at room temperature
2 teaspoons table salt
¼ cup sugar
1½ cups whole-wheat flour
2½ cups white bread flour
2¼ teaspoons bread machine yeast

<u>12 slice bread (1½ pounds)</u>
¾ cup lukewarm water
⅓ cup unsalted butter, melted
2 eggs, at room temperature
1½ teaspoons table salt
3 tablespoons sugar
1 cup whole-wheat flour
2 cups white bread flour
1⅔ teaspoons bread machine yeast

Directions

1. Choose the size of loaf you would like to make and measure your ingredients.
2. Add the ingredients to the bread pan in the order listed above.
3. Place the pan in the bread machine and close the lid.

4. Turn on the bread maker. Select the Whole Wheat/Wholegrain or White/Basic setting, wither one will work well for this recipe. Then select the loaf size, and finally the crust color. Start the cycle.
5. When the cycle is finished and the bread is baked, carefully remove the pan from the machine. Use a pot holder as the handle will be very hot. Let rest for a few minutes.
6. Remove the bread from the pan and allow to cool on a wire rack for at least 10 minutes before slicing.

Nutrition per slice
Calories 176, fat 5.3 g, carbs 24.2 g,
sodium 294 mg, protein 5.2 g

Oat Bran Nutmeg Bread

Makes 1 loaf

Ingredients

<u>16 slice bread (2 pounds)</u>
1 cup lukewarm water
3 tablespoons unsalted butter, melted
¼ cup blackstrap molasses
½ teaspoon table salt
3 cups whole-wheat bread flour
¼ teaspoon ground nutmeg
1 cup oat bran
2¼ teaspoons bread machine yeast

<u>12 slice bread (1½ pounds)</u>
¾ cup lukewarm water
2¼ tablespoons unsalted butter, melted
3 tablespoons blackstrap molasses
⅓ teaspoon table salt
2¼ cups whole-wheat bread flour
¼ teaspoon ground nutmeg
¾ cup oat bran
1⅔ teaspoons bread machine yeast

Directions

1. Choose the size of loaf you would like to make and measure your ingredients.
2. Add the ingredients to the bread pan in the order listed above.
3. Place the pan in the bread machine and close the lid.
4. Turn on the bread maker. Select the Whole Wheat/Wholegrain setting, then the loaf size, and finally the crust color. Start the cycle.

5. When the cycle is finished and the bread is baked, carefully remove the pan from the machine. Use a pot holder as the handle will be very hot. Let rest for a few minutes.
6. Remove the bread from the pan and allow to cool on a wire rack for at least 10 minutes before slicing.

Nutrition per slice
Calories 141, fat 2.8 g, carbs 23.6 g,
sodium 124 mg, protein 3.4 g

Multigrain Honey Bread

Makes 1 loaf

Ingredients

<u>16 slice bread (2 pounds)</u>
1½ cups lukewarm water
2 tablespoons unsalted butter, melted
1 tablespoon honey
1 teaspoon table salt
1½ cups multigrain flour
2¾ cups white bread flour
2 teaspoons bread machine yeast

<u>12 slice bread (1½ pounds)</u>
1⅛ cups lukewarm water
2 tablespoons unsalted butter, melted
1½ tablespoons honey
1½ teaspoons table salt
1⅛ cups multigrain flour
2 cups white bread flour
1½ teaspoons bread machine yeast

Directions

1. Choose the size of loaf you would like to make and measure your ingredients.
2. Add the ingredients to the bread pan in the order listed above.
3. Place the pan in the bread machine and close the lid.
4. Turn on the bread maker. Select the White/Basic setting, then the loaf size, and finally the crust color. Start the cycle.

5. When the cycle is finished and the bread is baked, carefully remove the pan from the machine. Use a pot holder as the handle will be very hot. Let rest for a few minutes.
6. Remove the bread from the pan and allow to cool on a wire rack for at least 10 minutes before slicing.

Nutrition per slice
Calories 144, fat 2.2 g, carbs 26.3 g,
sodium 287 mg, protein 4.1 g

Pumpernickel Bread

Makes 1 loaf

Ingredients

<u>16 slice bread (2 pounds)</u>
1 1/3 cups water, lukewarm between 80 and 90°F
2 large eggs, room temperature and not cold
¼ cup oil
¼ cup honey
3 tablespoons dry milk powder
¼ cup cocoa powder
3 tablespoons caraway seeds
1 tablespoon instant coffee granules
2 teaspoons table salt
1 cup rye flour
1 cup whole wheat bread flour
2 cups while bread flour
2 ¼ teaspoons bread machine yeast

<u>12 slice bread (1 ½ pounds)</u>
3/4 cups water, lukewarm between 80 and 90°F
2 large eggs, room temperature and not cold
2 tablespoons oil
2 tablespoons honey
3 tablespoons dry milk powder
3 tablespoons cocoa powder
2 tablespoons caraway seeds
2 teaspoon instant coffee granules
1 1/2 teaspoons table salt
3/4 cup rye flour
3/4 cup whole wheat bread flour
1 1/2 cups while bread flour
1 3/4 teaspoons bread machine yeast

Directions

1. Choose the size of loaf you would like to make and measure your ingredients. If you want to make a 1-pound or 2 ½-pound loaf, please adjust your ingredient quantities accordingly. You can look at the conversion table at the end of the book for easy adjustments or click here.
2. Take the bread pan; add the ingredients in order listed above.
3. Secure the pan into the bread machine and close the lid.
4. Power the bread maker and select the option of the bread – White/Basic – then the size of the loaf you are making, and finally the crust color you desire. Start the machine.
5. After the bread cycle is done and the bread is cooked, carefully remove the pan from the machine. Use a pot holder as the handle will be very hot. Let rest for a few minutes.
6. Remove the bread from the pan and allow to cool down on a wired rack for at least 10 minutes or more before slicing.

Nutrition per slice
Calories 134, fat 3.1 g, carbs 19 g, sodium 143 mg, protein 4.2 g

Classic Dark Bread

Makes 1 loaf

Ingredients

<u>16 slice bread (2 pounds)</u>
1¼ cups lukewarm water
2 tablespoons unsalted butter, melted
½ cup molasses
½ teaspoon table salt
1 cup rye flour
2½ cups white bread flour
2 tablespoons unsweetened cocoa powder
Pinch ground nutmeg
2¼ teaspoons bread machine yeast

<u>12 slice bread (1½ pounds)</u>
1 cup lukewarm water
1½ tablespoons unsalted butter, melted
⅓ cup molasses
⅓ teaspoon table salt
¾ cup rye flour
2 cups white bread flour
1½ tablespoons unsweetened cocoa powder
Pinch ground nutmeg
1⅔ teaspoons bread machine yeast

Directions
1. Choose the size of loaf you would like to make and measure your ingredients.
2. Add the ingredients to the bread pan in the order listed above.
3. Place the pan in the bread machine and close the lid.

4. Turn on the bread maker. Select the White/Basic setting, then the loaf size, and finally the crust color. Start the cycle.
5. When the cycle is finished and the bread is baked, carefully remove the pan from the machine. Use a pot holder as the handle will be very hot. Let rest for a few minutes.
6. Remove the bread from the pan and allow to cool on a wire rack for at least 10 minutes before slicing.

Nutrition per slice
Calories 143, fat 2.3 g, carbs 28.6 g,
sodium 237 mg, protein 3.8 g

Classic Corn Bread

Makes 1 loaf

Ingredients
<u>16 slice bread (2 pounds)</u>
1⅓ cups lukewarm buttermilk
⅓ cup unsalted butter, melted
2 eggs, at room temperature
⅓ cup sugar
1½ teaspoons table salt
1⅔ cups all-purpose flour
1⅓ cups cornmeal
1⅓ tablespoon baking powder

<u>12 slice bread (1½ pounds)</u>
1 cup lukewarm buttermilk
¼ cup unsalted butter, melted
2 eggs, at room temperature
¼ cup sugar
1 teaspoon table salt
1⅓ cups all-purpose flour
1 cup cornmeal
1 tablespoon baking powder

Directions
1. Choose the size of loaf you would like to make and measure your ingredients.
2. Add the ingredients to the bread pan in the order listed above.
3. Place the pan in the bread machine and close the lid.
4. Turn on the bread maker. Select the Quick/Rapid setting, then the loaf size, and finally the crust color. Start the cycle.

5. When the cycle is finished and the bread is baked, carefully remove the pan from the machine. Use a pot holder as the handle will be very hot. Let rest for a few minutes.
6. Remove the bread from the pan and allow to cool on a wire rack for at least 10 minutes before slicing.

Nutrition per slice
Calories 157, fat 5.2 g, carbs 23.8 g,
sodium 257 mg, protein 4.1 g

Basic Seed Bread

Makes 1 loaf

Ingredients

<u>16 slice bread (2 pounds)</u>
1½ cups lukewarm water
2 tablespoons unsalted butter, melted
2 tablespoons sugar
1½ teaspoons table salt
3¼ cups white bread flour
¾ cup ground chia seeds
2 tablespoons sesame seeds
2 teaspoons bread machine yeast

<u>12 slice bread (1½ pounds)</u>
1⅛ cups lukewarm water
1½ tablespoons unsalted butter, melted
1½ tablespoons sugar
1⅛ teaspoons table salt
2½ cups white bread flour
½ cup ground chia seeds
1½ tablespoons sesame seeds
1½ teaspoons bread machine yeast

Directions

1. Choose the size of loaf you would like to make and measure your ingredients.
2. Add the ingredients to the bread pan in the order listed above.
3. Place the pan in the bread machine and close the lid.
4. Turn on the bread maker. Select the White/Basic setting, then the loaf size, and finally the crust color. Start the cycle.

5. When the cycle is finished and the bread is baked, carefully remove the pan from the machine. Use a pot holder as the handle will be very hot. Let rest for a few minutes.
6. Remove the bread from the pan and allow to cool on a wire rack for at least 10 minutes before slicing.

Nutrition per slice
Calories 153, fat 2.3 g, carbs 24.8 g,
sodium 208 mg, protein 5.3 g

Basic Bulgur Bread

Makes 1 loaf

Ingredients

<u>16 slice bread (2 pounds)</u>
½ cup lukewarm water
½ cup bulgur wheat
1⅓ cups lukewarm milk
1⅓ tablespoons unsalted butter, melted
1⅓ tablespoons sugar
1 teaspoon table salt
4 cups bread flour
2 teaspoons bread machine yeast

<u>12 slice bread (1½ pounds)</u>
⅓ cup lukewarm water
⅓ cup bulgur wheat
1 cup lukewarm milk
1 tablespoon unsalted butter, melted
1 tablespoon sugar
¾ teaspoon table salt
3 cups bread flour
1½ teaspoons bread machine yeast

Directions

1. Choose the size of loaf you would like to make and measure your ingredients.
2. Add the water and bulgur wheat to the bread pan and set aside for 25–30 minutes for the bulgur wheat to soften.
3. Add the other ingredients to the bread pan in the order listed above.
4. Place the pan in the bread machine and close the lid.

5. Turn on the bread maker. Select the White/Basic setting, then the loaf size, and finally the crust color. Start the cycle.
6. When the cycle is finished and the bread is baked, carefully remove the pan from the machine. Use a pot holder as the handle will be very hot. Let rest for a few minutes.
7. Remove the bread from the pan and allow to cool on a wire rack for at least 10 minutes before slicing.

Nutrition per slice
Calories 160, fat 2.6 g, carbs 28.7 g, sodium 163 mg, protein 5 g

Oat Quinoa Bread

Makes 1 loaf

Ingredients

<u>16 slice bread (2 pounds)</u>
1⅓ cups lukewarm milk
¾ cup cooked quinoa, cooled
5 tablespoons unsalted butter, melted
4 teaspoons sugar
1⅓ teaspoons table salt
2 cups white bread flour
5 tablespoons quick oats
1 cup whole-wheat flour
2 teaspoons bread machine yeast

<u>12 slice bread (1½ pounds)</u>
1 cup lukewarm milk
⅔ cup cooked quinoa, cooled
¼ cup unsalted butter, melted
1 tablespoon sugar
1 teaspoon table salt
1½ cups white bread flour
¼ cup quick oats
¾ cup whole-wheat flour
1½ teaspoons bread machine yeast

Directions

1. Choose the size of loaf you would like to make and measure your ingredients.
2. Add the ingredients to the bread pan in the order listed above.
3. Place the pan in the bread machine and close the lid.

4. Turn on the bread maker. Select the White/Basic setting, then the loaf size, and finally the crust color. Start the cycle.
5. When the cycle is finished and the bread is baked, carefully remove the pan from the machine. Use a pot holder as the handle will be very hot. Let rest for a few minutes.
6. Remove the bread from the pan and allow to cool on a wire rack for at least 10 minutes before slicing.

Nutrition per slice
Calories 153, fat 5.3 g, carbs 22.3 g,
sodium 238 mg, protein 3.8 g

Whole Wheat Sunflower Bread

Makes 1 loaf

Ingredients
<u>16 slice bread (2 pounds)</u>
1⅛ cups lukewarm water
2 tablespoons honey
2 tablespoons unsalted butter, melted
1 teaspoon table salt
3 cups whole-wheat flour
1 cup white bread flour
2 tablespoons sesame seeds
¼ cup raw sunflower seeds
2¼ teaspoons bread machine yeast

<u>12 slice bread (1½ pounds)</u>
1 cup lukewarm water
1½ tablespoons honey
1½ tablespoons unsalted butter, melted
¾ teaspoon table salt
2½ cups whole-wheat flour
¾ cup white bread flour
1 tablespoon sesame seeds
3 tablespoons raw sunflower seeds
1½ teaspoons bread machine yeast

Directions
1. Choose the size of loaf you would like to make and measure your ingredients.
2. Add the ingredients to the bread pan in the order listed above.
3. Place the pan in the bread machine and close the lid.

4. Turn on the bread maker. Select the Whole Wheat/Wholegrain setting, then the loaf size, and finally the crust color. Start the cycle.
5. When the cycle is finished and the bread is baked, carefully remove the pan from the machine. Use a pot holder as the handle will be very hot. Let rest for a few minutes.
6. Remove the bread from the pan and allow to cool on a wire rack for at least 10 minutes before slicing.

Nutrition per slice
Calories 253, fat 3.3 g, carbs 27.4 g, sodium 154 mg, protein 4.2 g

Honey Sunflower Bread

Makes 1 loaf

Ingredients

<u>16 slice bread (2 pounds)</u>
1⅓ cups lukewarm water
2 eggs, at room temperature
¼ cup unsalted butter, melted
¼ cup skim milk powder
2 tablespoons honey
2 teaspoons table salt
4 cups white bread flour
1 cup raw sunflower seeds
1¾ teaspoons bread machine yeast

<u>12 slice bread (1½ pounds)</u>
1 cup lukewarm water
1 egg, at room temperature
3 tablespoons unsalted butter, melted
3 tablespoons skim milk powder
1½ tablespoons honey
1½ teaspoons table salt
3 cups white bread flour
¾ cup raw sunflower seeds
1 teaspoon bread machine yeast

Directions

1. Choose the size of loaf you would like to make and measure your ingredients.
2. Add the ingredients to the bread pan in the order listed above.
3. Place the pan in the bread machine and close the lid.

4. Turn on the bread maker. Select the White/Basic setting, then the loaf size, and finally the crust color. Start the cycle.
5. When the cycle is finished and the bread is baked, carefully remove the pan from the machine. Use a pot holder as the handle will be very hot. Let rest for a few minutes.
6. Remove the bread from the pan and allow to cool on a wire rack for at least 10 minutes before slicing.

Nutrition per slice
Calories 172, fat 4.7 g, carbs 27.8 g,
sodium 324 mg, protein 4.9 g

Flaxseed Milk Bread

Makes 1 loaf

Ingredients

<u>16 slice bread (2 pounds)</u>
1½ cups lukewarm milk
2 tablespoons unsalted butter, melted
2 tablespoons honey
2 teaspoons table salt
4 cups white bread flour
½ cup flaxseed
1½ teaspoons bread machine yeast

<u>12 slice bread (1½ pounds)</u>
1⅛ cups lukewarm milk
1½ tablespoons unsalted butter, melted
1½ tablespoons honey
1 teaspoon table salt
3 cups white bread flour
¼ cup flaxseed
1¼ teaspoons bread machine yeast

Directions

1. Choose the size of loaf you would like to make and measure your ingredients.
2. Add the ingredients to the bread pan in the order listed above.
3. Place the pan in the bread machine and close the lid.
4. Turn on the bread maker. Select the White/Basic setting, then the loaf size, and finally the crust color. Start the cycle.

5. When the cycle is finished and the bread is baked, carefully remove the pan from the machine. Use a pot holder as the handle will be very hot. Let rest for a few minutes.
6. Remove the bread from the pan and allow to cool on a wire rack for at least 10 minutes before slicing.

Nutrition per slice
Calories 147, fat 3.2 g, carbs 27.4 g,
sodium 216 mg, protein 5.8 g

Honey Wheat Bread

Makes 1 loaf

Ingredients

<u>16 slice bread (2 pounds)</u>
1⅔ cups boiling water
¼ cup + 4 teaspoons cracked wheat
¼ cup + 4 teaspoons unsalted butter, melted
¼ cup honey
2 teaspoons table salt
1⅓ cups whole-wheat flour
2⅔ cups white bread flour
2½ teaspoons bread machine yeast

<u>12 slice bread (1½ pounds)</u>
1¼ cups boiling water
¼ cup cracked wheat
¼ cup unsalted butter, melted
3 tablespoons honey
1½ teaspoons table salt
1 cup whole-wheat flour
2 cups white bread flour
2 teaspoons bread machine yeast

Directions
1. Choose the size of loaf you would like to make and measure your ingredients.
2. Add the boiling water and cracked wheat to the bread pan; set aside for 25–30 minutes for the wheat to soften.
3. Add the other ingredients to the bread pan in the order listed above.
4. Place the pan in the bread machine and close the lid.

5. Turn on the bread maker. Select the White/Basic setting, then the loaf size, and finally the crust color. Start the cycle.
6. When the cycle is finished and the bread is baked, carefully remove the pan from the machine. Use a pot holder as the handle will be very hot. Let rest for a few minutes.
7. Remove the bread from the pan and allow to cool on a wire rack for at least 10 minutes before slicing.

Nutrition per slice
Calories 168, fat 4.3 g, carbs 31.3 g,
sodium 296 mg, protein 4.1 g

French Crusty Loaf Bread

Makes 1 loaf

Ingredients
16 slice bread (2 pounds)
2 cups + 2 tablespoon water, lukewarm between 80 and 90°F
4 teaspoons sugar
2 teaspoons table salt
6 1/2 cups white bread flour
2 teaspoons bread machine yeast

12 slice bread (1 ½ pounds)
1 1/2 cups + 1 tablespoon water, lukewarm between 80 and 90°F
3 teaspoons sugar
1 1/2 teaspoons table salt
4 3/4 cups white bread flour
1 1/2 teaspoons bread machine yeast

Directions
1. Choose the size of loaf you would like to make and measure your ingredients.
2. Add the ingredients to the bread pan in the order listed above.
3. Place the pan in the bread machine and close the lid.
4. Turn on the bread maker. Select the French setting, then the loaf size, and finally the crust color. Start the cycle.
5. When the cycle is finished and the bread is baked, carefully remove the pan from the machine. Use a pot holder as the handle will be very hot. Let rest for a few minutes.
6. Remove the bread from the pan and allow to cool on a wire rack for at least 10 minutes before slicing.

Nutrition per slice
Calories 186, fat 1.2 g, carbs 31.4 g,

sodium 126 mg, protein 5.7 g

GLUTEN FREE BREADS

Classic White Bread

Makes 1 loaf

Ingredients
16 slice bread (2 pounds)
1½ cups lukewarm water
¼ cup canola oil
1 teaspoon apple cider vinegar
3 eggs, room temperature, slightly beaten
2 cups white rice flour
½ cup tapioca flour
⅔ cup nonfat dry milk powder
½ cup potato starch
⅓ cup cornstarch
3 tablespoons sugar
1 tablespoon xanthan gum
1 teaspoon table salt
2 teaspoons bread machine yeast

12 slice bread (1½ pounds)
1¼ cup lukewarm water
3 tablespoons canola oil
¾ teaspoon apple cider vinegar
2 eggs, room temperature, slightly beaten
1½ cups white rice flour
⅔ cup tapioca flour
½ cup nonfat dry milk powder
½ cup potato starch
⅓ cup cornstarch
2 tablespoon sugar

⅔ tablespoon xanthan gum
⅔ teaspoon table salt
1¼ teaspoons bread machine yeast

Directions

1. Choose the size of loaf you would like to make and measure your ingredients.
2. Add the ingredients to the bread pan in the order listed above.
3. Place the pan in the bread machine and close the lid.
4. Turn on the bread maker. Select the White/Basic or Gluten-Free (if your machine has this setting) setting, then the loaf size, and finally the crust color. Start the cycle.
5. When the cycle is finished and the bread is baked, carefully remove the pan from the machine. Use a pot holder as the handle will be very hot. Let rest for a few minutes.
6. Remove the bread from the pan and allow to cool on a wire rack for at least 10 minutes before slicing.

Nutrition per slice
Calories 163, fat 4.2 g, carbs 28 g, sodium 176 mg, protein 4.3 g

Pecan Apple Spice Bread

Makes 1 loaf

Ingredients
<u>16 slice bread (2 pounds)</u>
½ cup lukewarm water
3 tablespoons canola oil
1 teaspoon apple cider vinegar
3 tablespoons light brown sugar, packed
1 cup Granny Smith apples, grated
3 eggs, room temperature, slightly beaten
¾ cup brown rice flour
¾ cup tapioca flour
¾ cup millet flour
½ cup corn starch
2 tablespoons apple pie spice
1 tablespoon xanthan gum
1 teaspoon table salt
2 teaspoons bread machine yeast
½ cup pecans, chopped

<u>12 slice bread (1½ pounds)</u>
⅓ cup lukewarm water
2¼ tablespoons canola oil
¾ teaspoon apple cider vinegar
2¼ tablespoons light brown sugar, packed
¾ cup Granny Smith apples, grated
2 eggs, room temperature, slightly beaten
½ cup brown rice flour
½ cup tapioca flour
½ cup millet flour
⅓ cup corn starch
1½ tablespoons apple pie spice

¾ tablespoon xanthan gum
¾ teaspoon table salt
1¼ teaspoons bread machine yeast
⅓ cup pecans, chopped

Directions
1. Choose the size of loaf you would like to make and measure your ingredients.
2. Add all of the ingredients except for the pecans to the bread pan in the order listed above.
3. Place the pan in the bread machine and close the lid.
4. Turn on the bread maker. Select the White/Basic or Gluten-Free (if your machine has this setting) setting, then the loaf size, and finally the crust color. Start the cycle.
5. When the machine signals to add ingredients, add the chopped pecans.
6. When the cycle is finished and the bread is baked, carefully remove the pan from the machine. Use a pot holder as the handle will be very hot. Let rest for a few minutes.
7. Remove the bread from the pan and allow to cool on a wire rack for at least 10 minutes before slicing.

Nutrition per slice
Calories 154, fat 5 g, carbs 22.3 g, sodium 174 mg, protein 3.1 g

Pumpkin Jalapeno Bread

Makes 1 loaf

Ingredients

<u>16 slice bread (2 pounds)</u>
¾ cup lukewarm water
2 large eggs, beaten
½ cup pumpkin puree
3 tablespoons honey
2½ tablespoons vegetable oil
1 teaspoon apple cider vinegar
2 teaspoons sugar
1 teaspoon table salt
¾ cup brown rice flour
¾ cup tapioca flour
½ cup corn starch
½ cup yellow corn meal
1 tablespoon xanthan gum
1 medium jalapeno pepper, seeded and deveined
2 teaspoons crushed red pepper flakes
2 teaspoons bread machine yeast

<u>12 slice bread (1½ pounds)</u>
½ cup lukewarm water
2 medium eggs, beaten
⅓ cup pumpkin puree
2¼ tablespoons honey
1½ tablespoons vegetable oil
¾ teaspoon apple cider vinegar
1½ teaspoons sugar
¾ teaspoon table salt
½ cup brown rice flour
½ cup tapioca flour

⅓ cup corn starch
⅓ cup yellow corn meal
¾ tablespoon xanthan gum
1 small jalapeno pepper, seeded and deveined
1½ teaspoons crushed red pepper flakes
1¼ teaspoons bread machine yeast

Directions

1. Choose the size of loaf you would like to make and measure your ingredients.
2. Add the ingredients to the bread pan in the order listed above.
3. Place the pan in the bread machine and close the lid.
4. Turn on the bread maker. Select the White/Basic or Gluten-Free (if your machine has this setting) setting, then the loaf size, and finally the crust color. Start the cycle.
5. When the cycle is finished and the bread is baked, carefully remove the pan from the machine. Use a pot holder as the handle will be very hot. Let rest for a few minutes.
6. Remove the bread from the pan and allow to cool on a wire rack for at least 10 minutes before slicing.

Nutrition per slice
Calories 124, fat 2.3 g, carbs 21.7 g, sodium 179 mg, protein 2 g

Walnut Banana Bread

Makes 1 loaf

Ingredients

<u>16 slice bread (2 pounds)</u>
½ cup lukewarm water
3 tablespoons canola oil
1 teaspoon apple cider vinegar
2 eggs, beaten
2 small banana, mashed
1 teaspoon table salt
¾ cup brown rice flour
¾ cup white rice flour
¾ cup amaranth flour
½ cup corn starch
1 tablespoon xanthan gum
1 teaspoon cinnamon
½ teaspoon nutmeg
2 teaspoons bread machine yeast
1 cup walnuts, chopped

<u>12 slice bread (1½ pounds)</u>
⅓ cup lukewarm water
2 tablespoons canola oil
¾ teaspoon apple cider vinegar
2 eggs, beaten
1½ small bananas, mashed
¾ teaspoon table salt
½ cup brown rice flour
½ cup white rice flour
½ cup amaranth flour
⅓ cup corn starch
¾ tablespoon xanthan gum

¾ teaspoon cinnamon
⅓ teaspoon nutmeg
1½ teaspoons bread machine yeast
¾ cup walnuts, chopped

Directions
1. Choose the size of loaf you would like to make and measure your ingredients.
2. Add the ingredients to the bread pan in the order listed above.
3. Place the pan in the bread machine and close the lid.
4. Turn on the bread maker. Select the Quick/Rapid setting, then the loaf size, and finally the crust color. Start the cycle.
5. When the cycle is finished and the bread is baked, carefully remove the pan from the machine. Use a pot holder as the handle will be very hot. Let rest for a few minutes.
6. Remove the bread from the pan and allow to cool on a wire rack for at least 10 minutes before slicing.

Nutrition per slice
Calories 193, fat 8.3 g, carbs 24.4 g,
sodium 172 mg, protein 4.2 g

Basic Honey Bread

Makes 1 loaf

Ingredients
16 slice bread (2 pounds)
2 cups warm milk
⅓ cup unsalted butter, melted
2 eggs, beaten
1¼ teaspoons apple cider vinegar
⅔ cup honey
1¼ teaspoons table salt
4 cups gluten-free flour(s) of your choice
2 teaspoons xanthan gum
2 teaspoons bread machine yeast

12 slice bread (1½ pounds)
1½ cups warm milk
¼ cup unsalted butter, melted
2 eggs, beaten
1 teaspoon apple cider vinegar
½ cup honey
1 teaspoon table salt
3 cups gluten-free flour(s) of your choice
1½ teaspoons xanthan gum
1¾ teaspoons bread machine yeast

Directions
1. Choose the size of loaf you would like to make and measure your ingredients.
2. Add the ingredients to the bread pan in the order listed above.
3. Place the pan in the bread machine and close the lid.

4. Turn on the bread maker. Select the White/Basic or Gluten-Free (if your machine has this setting) setting, then the loaf size, and finally the crust color. Start the cycle.
5. When the cycle is finished and the bread is baked, carefully remove the pan from the machine. Use a pot holder as the handle will be very hot. Let rest for a few minutes.
6. Remove the bread from the pan and allow to cool on a wire rack for at least 10 minutes before slicing.

Nutrition per slice
Calories 212, fat 6.2 g, carbs 34.4 g,
sodium 243 mg, protein 4.9 g

Onion Buttermilk Bread

Makes 1 loaf

Ingredients

<u>16 slice bread (2 pounds)</u>
1¼ cups lukewarm water
¼ cup unsalted butter, melted
1 teaspoon apple cider vinegar
¼ cup dry buttermilk powder
3 large eggs, beaten
¼ cup sugar
1½ teaspoons table salt
½ cup potato flour
½ cup tapioca flour
2 cup white rice flour
1 tablespoon dill, chopped
¼ cup green onion, chopped
3½ teaspoons xanthan gum
2¼ teaspoons bread machine yeast

<u>12 slice bread (1½ pounds)</u>
1 cup lukewarm water
3 tablespoons unsalted butter, melted
¾ teaspoon apple cider vinegar
3 tablespoons dry buttermilk powder
3 medium eggs, beaten
3 tablespoons sugar
1 teaspoon table salt
⅓ cup potato flour
⅓ cup tapioca flour
1½ cups white rice flour
¾ tablespoon dill, chopped
3 tablespoons green onion, chopped

2⅔ teaspoons xanthan gum
1½ teaspoons bread machine yeast

Directions
1. Choose the size of loaf you would like to make and measure your ingredients.
2. Add the ingredients to the bread pan in the order listed above.
3. Place the pan in the bread machine and close the lid.
4. Turn on the bread maker. Select the White/Basic or Gluten-Free (if your machine has this setting) setting, then the loaf size, and finally the crust color. Start the cycle.
5. When the cycle is finished and the bread is baked, carefully remove the pan from the machine. Use a pot holder as the handle will be very hot. Let rest for a few minutes.
6. Remove the bread from the pan and allow to cool on a wire rack for at least 10 minutes before slicing.

Nutrition per slice
Calories 173, fat 4.1 g, carbs 28.6 g,
sodium 209 mg, protein 3.3 g

Pecan Cranberry Bread

Makes 1 loaf

Ingredients
<u>16 slice bread (2 pounds)</u>
1½ cups lukewarm water
¼ cup canola oil
1 tablespoon orange zest
1 teaspoon apple cider vinegar
3 eggs, slightly beaten
3 tablespoons sugar
1 teaspoon table salt
2 cup white rice flour
⅔ cup nonfat dry milk powder
½ cup tapioca flour
½ cup potato starch
⅓ cup corn starch
1 tablespoon xanthan gum
2 teaspoons bread machine yeast
⅔ cup dried cranberries
⅔ cup pecan pieces

<u>12 slice bread (1½ pounds)</u>
1⅛ cups lukewarm water
3 tablespoons canola oil
¾ tablespoon orange zest
¾ teaspoon apple cider vinegar
2 eggs, slightly beaten
2¼ tablespoons sugar
¾ teaspoon table salt
1½ cups white rice flour
½ cup nonfat dry milk powder
⅓ cup tapioca flour

⅓ cup potato starch
¼ cup corn starch
¾ tablespoon xanthan gum
1½ teaspoons bread machine yeast
½ cup dried cranberries
½ cup pecan pieces

Directions
1. Choose the size of loaf you would like to make and measure your ingredients.
2. Add all of the ingredients except for the pecans and cranberries to the bread pan in the order listed above.
3. Place the pan in the bread machine and close the lid.
4. Turn on the bread maker. Select the Gluten Free or Fruit/Nut (if your machine has this setting) setting, then the loaf size, and finally the crust color. Start the cycle. (If you don't have either of the above settings, use Basic/White.)
5. When the machine signals to add ingredients, add the pecans and cranberries. (Some machines have a fruit/nut hopper where you can add the pecans and cranberries when you start the machine. The machine will automatically add them to the dough during the baking process.)
6. When the cycle is finished and the bread is baked, carefully remove the pan from the machine. Use a pot holder as the handle will be very hot. Let rest for a few minutes.
7. Remove the bread from the pan and allow to cool on a wire rack for at least 10 minutes before slicing.

Nutrition per slice
Calories 228, fat 6.7 g, carbs 31.3 g,
sodium 189 mg, protein 3.8 g

Cheese Potato Bread

Makes 1 loaf

Ingredients
<u>16 slice bread (2 pounds)</u>
1¼ cups lukewarm water
3 tablespoons vegetable oil
3 large eggs, beaten
½ cup dry skim milk powder
¼ cup sugar
1 teaspoon apple cider vinegar
1½ teaspoons table salt
½ cup cornstarch
¾ cup cottage cheese
¼ cup snipped chives
½ cup instant potato buds
½ cup potato starch
½ cup tapioca flour
2 cups white rice flour
2¼ teaspoons bread machine yeast

<u>12 slice bread (1½ pounds)</u>
1 cup lukewarm water
2¼ tablespoons vegetable oil
2 large eggs, beaten
⅓ cup dry skim milk powder
3 tablespoons sugar
¾ teaspoon apple cider vinegar
1⅛ teaspoons table salt
⅓ cup cornstarch
½ cup cottage cheese
3 tablespoons snipped chives
⅓ cup instant potato buds

⅓ cup potato starch
⅓ cup tapioca flour
1½ cups white rice flour
1½ teaspoons bread machine yeast

Directions
1. Choose the size of loaf you would like to make and measure your ingredients.
2. Add the ingredients to the bread pan in the order listed above.
3. Place the pan in the bread machine and close the lid.
4. Turn on the bread maker. Select the White/Basic or Gluten-Free (if your machine has this setting) setting, then the loaf size, and finally the crust color. Start the cycle.
5. When the cycle is finished and the bread is baked, carefully remove the pan from the machine. Use a pot holder as the handle will be very hot. Let rest for a few minutes.
6. Remove the bread from the pan and allow to cool on a wire rack for at least 10 minutes before slicing.

Nutrition per slice
Calories 197, fat 4.6 g, carbs 27.1 g, sodium 230 mg, protein 5.2 g

Instant Cocoa Bread

Makes 1 loaf

Ingredients

<u>16 slice bread (2 pounds)</u>
1½ cups lukewarm water
3 large eggs, beaten
3 tablespoons molasses
2 tablespoons canola oil
1 teaspoon apple cider vinegar
3 tablespoons light brown sugar
1½ teaspoons table salt
2 cups white rice flour
⅔ cup potato starch
⅓ cup tapioca flour
2½ teaspoons xanthan gum
2 teaspoons cocoa powder
2 teaspoons instant coffee granules
3 teaspoons bread machine yeast

<u>12 slice bread (1½ pounds)</u>
1⅛ cups lukewarm water
2 large eggs, beaten
2¼ tablespoons molasses
1½ tablespoons canola oil
¾ teaspoon apple cider vinegar
2¼ tablespoons light brown sugar
1⅛ teaspoons table salt
1½ cups white rice flour
½ cup potato starch
¼ cup tapioca flour
1½ teaspoons xanthan gum
1½ teaspoons cocoa powder

1½ teaspoons instant coffee granules
2 teaspoons bread machine yeast

Directions
1. Choose the size of loaf you would like to make and measure your ingredients.
2. Add the ingredients to the bread pan in the order listed above.
3. Place the pan in the bread machine and close the lid.
4. Turn on the bread maker. Select the White/Basic or Gluten-Free (if your machine has this setting) setting, then the loaf size, and finally the crust color. Start the cycle.
5. When the cycle is finished and the bread is baked, carefully remove the pan from the machine. Use a pot holder as the handle will be very hot. Let rest for a few minutes.
6. Remove the bread from the pan and allow to cool on a wire rack for at least 10 minutes before slicing.

Nutrition per slice
Calories 146, fat 3.2 g, carbs 26.4 g,
sodium 166 mg, protein 2.6 g

Mix Seed Bread

Makes 1 loaf

Ingredients

<u>16 slice bread (2 pounds)</u>
2¼ cups lukewarm milk
½ cup + 1 tablespoon cooking oil
1½ teaspoons vinegar
3 eggs, slightly beaten
1½ tablespoons sugar
1½ teaspoons table salt
3½ cups gluten-free flour(s) of your choice
3 tablespoons poppy seeds
3 tablespoons pumpkin seeds
3 tablespoons sunflower seeds
3 teaspoons bread machine yeast

<u>12 slice bread (1½ pounds)</u>
2 cups lukewarm milk
6 tablespoons cooking oil
1 teaspoon vinegar
2 eggs, slightly beaten
1 tablespoon sugar
1 teaspoon table salt
2⅔ cups gluten-free flour(s) of your choice
2 tablespoons poppy seeds
2 tablespoons pumpkin seeds
2 tablespoons sunflower seeds
2 teaspoons bread machine yeast

Directions

1. Choose the size of loaf you would like to make and measure your ingredients.
2. Add the ingredients to the bread pan in the order listed above.
3. Place the pan in the bread machine and close the lid.
4. Turn on the bread maker. Select the White/Basic or Gluten-Free (if your machine has this setting) setting, then the loaf size, and finally the crust color. Start the cycle.
5. When the cycle is finished and the bread is baked, carefully remove the pan from the machine. Use a pot holder as the handle will be very hot. Let rest for a few minutes.
6. Remove the bread from the pan and allow to cool on a wire rack for at least 10 minutes before slicing.

Nutrition per slice

Calories 126, fat 8.3 g, carbs 14.6 g, sodium 233 mg, protein 4.2 g

Garlic Parsley Bread

Makes 1 loaf

Ingredients
<u>16 slice bread (2 pounds)</u>
1½ cups almond or coconut milk
¼ cup flax meal
12 tablespoons warm water
4 tablespoon butter
3 tablespoons maple syrup
3 teaspoon apple cider vinegar
¼ cup parsley, loosely chopped
10–12 cloves garlic, minced
1 teaspoon table salt
3¼ cups brown rice flour
½ cup corn starch
¼ cup potato starch
3 teaspoons xanthan gum
2 tablespoons garlic powder
2 tablespoons onion powder
2 teaspoons bread machine yeast

<u>12 slice bread (1½ pounds)</u>
1¼ cups almond or coconut milk
3 tablespoons flax meal
½ cup + 1 tablespoon warm water
3 tablespoons butter
2¼ tablespoons maple syrup
2¼ teaspoons apple cider vinegar
3 tablespoons parsley, loosely chopped
8–9 cloves garlic, minced
¾ teaspoon table salt
6 tablespoons + 2 teaspoons brown rice flour

⅓ cup corn starch
3 tablespoons potato starch
2 teaspoons xanthan gum
1½ tablespoons garlic powder
1½ tablespoons onion powder
1½ teaspoons bread machine yeast

Directions

1. Combine the water and flax meal in a bowl; set aside for 5–10 minutes to mix well.
2. Choose the size of loaf you would like to make and measure your ingredients.
3. Add the ingredients to the bread pan in the order listed above, including the flax meal.
4. Place the pan in the bread machine and close the lid.
5. Turn on the bread maker. Select the White/Basic or Gluten-Free (if your machine has this setting) setting, then the loaf size, and finally the crust color. Start the cycle.
6. When the cycle is finished and the bread is baked, carefully remove the pan from the machine. Use a pot holder as the handle will be very hot. Let rest for a few minutes.
7. Remove the bread from the pan and allow to cool on a wire rack for at least 10 minutes before slicing.

Nutrition per slice

Calories 193, fat 4.8 g, carbs 31.4 g,
sodium 201 mg, protein 3.4 g

Italian Herb Bread

Makes 1 loaf

Ingredients

<u>16 slice bread (2 pounds)</u>
3⅓ cups lukewarm water
3 eggs, beaten
⅓ cup vegetable oil
2 teaspoons table salt
¼ cup sugar
1¼ cups white bean flour
1¼ tablespoons mixed Italian herbs, dried
1¼ cups white rice flour
1¼ cups potato starch
⅔ cup tapioca flour
1⅓ tablespoons xanthan gum
2⅔–3 teaspoons bread machine yeast

<u>12 slice bread (1½ pounds)</u>
1½ cups lukewarm water
3 eggs, beaten
¼ cup vegetable oil
1½ teaspoons table salt
3 tablespoons sugar
1 cup white bean flour
1 tablespoon mixed Italian herbs, dried
1 cup white rice flour
1 cup potato starch
½ cup tapioca flour
1 tablespoon xanthan gum
2¼ teaspoons bread machine yeast

Directions

1. Choose the size of loaf you would like to make and measure your ingredients.
2. Add the ingredients to the bread pan in the order listed above.
3. Place the pan in the bread machine and close the lid.
4. Turn on the bread maker. Select the White/Basic or Gluten-Free (if your machine has this setting) setting, then the loaf size, and finally the crust color. Start the cycle.
5. When the cycle is finished and the bread is baked, carefully remove the pan from the machine. Use a pot holder as the handle will be very hot. Let rest for a few minutes.
6. Remove the bread from the pan and allow to cool on a wire rack for at least 10 minutes before slicing.

Nutrition per slice

Calories 188, fat 6.3 g, carbs 32.5 g,
sodium 306 mg, protein 3.4 g

FRUIT BREADS

Cinnamon Apple Bread

Makes 1 loaf

Ingredients

<u>16 slice bread (2 pounds)</u>
1⅓ cups lukewarm milk
3⅓ tablespoons butter, melted
2⅔ tablespoons sugar
2 teaspoons table salt
1⅓ teaspoons cinnamon, ground
A pinch ground cloves
4 cups white bread flour
2¼ teaspoons bread machine yeast
1⅓ cups peeled apple, finely diced

<u>12 slice bread (1½ pounds)</u>
1 cup lukewarm milk
2½ tablespoons butter, melted
2 tablespoons sugar
1½ teaspoons table salt
1 teaspoon cinnamon, ground
Pinch ground cloves
3 cups white bread flour
2¼ teaspoons bread machine yeast
1 cup peeled apple, finely diced

Directions

1. Choose the size of loaf you would like to make and measure your ingredients.
2. Add all of the ingredients except for the apples to the bread pan in the order listed above.
3. Place the pan in the bread machine and close the lid.
4. Turn on the bread maker. Select the White/Basic or Fruit/Nut (if your machine has this setting) setting, then the loaf size, and finally the crust color. Start the cycle.
5. When the machine signals to add ingredients, add the apples. (Some machines have a fruit/nut hopper where you can add the apples when you start the machine. The machine will automatically add them to the dough during the baking process.)
6. When the cycle is finished and the bread is baked, carefully remove the pan from the machine. Use a pot holder as the handle will be very hot. Let rest for a few minutes.
7. Remove the bread from the pan and allow to cool on a wire rack for at least 10 minutes before slicing.

Nutrition per slice

Calories 174, fat 2.3 g, carbs 26.4 g,
sodium 286 mg, protein 4.6 g

Blueberry Honey Bread

Makes 1 loaf

Ingredients

<u>16 slice bread (2 pounds)</u>
1 cup plain yogurt
⅔ cup lukewarm water
¼ cup honey
4 teaspoons unsalted butter, melted
2 teaspoons table salt
1½ teaspoons lime zest
⅔ teaspoon lemon extract
4 cups white bread flour
2¼ teaspoons bread machine yeast
1⅓ cups dried blueberries

<u>12 slice bread (1½ pounds)</u>
¾ cup plain yogurt
½ cup lukewarm water
3 tablespoons honey
1 tablespoon unsalted butter, melted
1½ teaspoons table salt
1 teaspoon lime zest
½ teaspoon lemon extract
3 cups white bread flour
2¼ teaspoons bread machine yeast
1 cup dried blueberries

Directions
1. Choose the size of loaf you would like to make and measure your ingredients.
2. Add all of the ingredients except for the blueberries to the bread pan in the order listed above.
3. Place the pan in the bread machine and close the lid.
4. Turn on the bread maker. Select the White/Basic or Fruit/Nut (if your machine has this setting) setting, then the loaf size, and finally the crust color. Start the cycle.
5. When the machine signals to add ingredients, add the blueberries. (Some machines have a fruit/nut hopper where you can add the blueberries when you start the machine. The machine will automatically add them to the dough during the baking process.)
6. When the cycle is finished and the bread is baked, carefully remove the pan from the machine. Use a pot holder as the handle will be very hot. Let rest for a few minutes.
7. Remove the bread from the pan and allow to cool on a wire rack for at least 10 minutes before slicing.

Nutrition per slice
Calories 153, fat 2.3 g, carbs 28.7 g,
sodium 286 mg, protein 5 g

Raisin Candied Fruit Bread

Makes 1 loaf

Ingredients

<u>16 slice bread (2 pounds)</u>
1 egg, beaten
1½ cups + 1 tablespoon lukewarm water
⅔ teaspoon ground cardamom
1¼ teaspoons table salt
2 tablespoons sugar
⅓ cup butter, melted
4 cups bread flour
1¼ teaspoons bread machine yeast
½ cup raisins
½ cup mixed candied fruit

<u>12 slice bread (1½ pounds)</u>
1 egg, beaten
1⅛ cup lukewarm water
½ teaspoon ground cardamom
1 teaspoon table salt
1½ tablespoons sugar
¼ cup butter, melted
3 cups bread flour
1 teaspoon bread machine yeast
⅓ cup raisins
⅓ cup mixed candied fruit

Directions

1. Choose the size of loaf you would like to make and measure your ingredients.
2. Add all of the ingredients except for the candied fruits and raisins to the bread pan in the order listed above.
3. Place the pan in the bread machine and close the lid.
4. Turn on the bread maker. Select the White/Basic or Fruit/Nut (if your machine has this setting) setting, then the loaf size, and finally the crust color. Start the cycle.
5. When the machine signals to add ingredients, add the candied fruits and raisins. (Some machines have a fruit/nut hopper where you can add the fruits and raisins when you start the machine. The machine will automatically add them to the dough during the baking process.)
6. When the cycle is finished and the bread is baked, carefully remove the pan from the machine. Use a pot holder as the handle will be very hot. Let rest for a few minutes.
7. Remove the bread from the pan and allow to cool on a wire rack for at least 10 minutes before slicing.

Nutrition per slice

Calories 206, fat 4.6 g, carbs 33.4 g, sodium 214 mg, protein 4.7 g

Spice Peach Bread

Makes 1 loaf

Ingredients

<u>16 slice bread (2 pounds)</u>
½ cup lukewarm heavy whipping cream
1 egg, beaten
1½ tablespoons unsalted butter, melted
3 tablespoons sugar
1½ teaspoons table salt
¼ teaspoon nutmeg, ground
½ teaspoon cinnamon, ground
3½ cups white bread flour
½ cup whole-wheat flour
1½ teaspoons bread machine yeast
1 cup canned peaches, drained and chopped

<u>12 slice bread (1½ pounds)</u>
⅓ cup lukewarm heavy whipping cream
1 egg, beaten
1 tablespoon unsalted butter, melted
2¼ tablespoons sugar
1⅛ teaspoons table salt
⅛ teaspoon nutmeg, ground
⅓ teaspoon cinnamon, ground
2⅔ cups white bread flour
⅓ cup whole-wheat flour
1⅛ teaspoons bread machine yeast
¾ cup canned peaches, drained and chopped

Directions

1. Choose the size of loaf you would like to make and measure your ingredients.
2. Add all of the ingredients except for the peach to the bread pan in the order listed above.
3. Place the pan in the bread machine and close the lid.
4. Turn on the bread maker. Select the White/Basic or Fruit/Nut (if your machine has this setting) setting, then the loaf size, and finally the crust color. Start the machine.
5. When the machine signals to add ingredients, add the peaches. (Some machines have a fruit/nut hopper where you can add the peaches when you start the machine. The machine will automatically add them to the dough during the baking process.)
6. When the cycle is finished and the bread is baked, carefully remove the pan from the machine. Use a pot holder as the handle will be very hot. Let rest for a few minutes.
7. Remove the bread from the pan and allow to cool on a wire rack for at least 10 minutes before slicing.

Nutrition per slice
Calories 157, fat 3.1 g, carbs 26.4 g, sodium 197 mg, protein 4.2 g

Cocoa Date Bread

Makes 1 loaf

Ingredients

<u>16 slice bread (2 pounds)</u>
1 cup lukewarm water
½ cup lukewarm milk
2 tablespoons unsalted butter, melted
5 tablespoons honey
3 tablespoons molasses
1 tablespoon sugar
3 tablespoons skim milk powder
1 teaspoon table salt
2 cups white bread flour
2½ cups whole-wheat flour
1 tablespoon cocoa powder, unsweetened
1½ teaspoons bread machine yeast
1 cup dates, chopped

<u>12 slice bread (1½ pounds)</u>
¾ cup lukewarm water
½ cup lukewarm milk
2 tablespoons unsalted butter, melted
¼ cup honey
3 tablespoons molasses
1 tablespoon sugar
2 tablespoons skim milk powder
1 teaspoon table salt
1¼ cups white bread flour
2¼ cups whole-wheat flour
1 tablespoon cocoa powder, unsweetened
1½ teaspoons bread machine yeast
¾ cup dates, chopped

Directions

1. Choose the size of loaf you would like to make and measure your ingredients.
2. Add all of the ingredients except for the dates to the bread pan in the order listed above.
3. Place the pan in the bread machine and close the lid.
4. Turn on the bread maker. Select the White/Basic or Fruit/Nut (if your machine has this setting) setting, then the loaf size, and finally the crust color. Start the cycle.
5. When the machine signals to add ingredients, add the dates. (Some machines have a fruit/nut hopper where you can add the dates when you start the machine. The machine will automatically add them to the dough during the baking process.)
6. When the cycle is finished and the bread is baked, carefully remove the pan from the machine. Use a pot holder as the handle will be very hot. Let rest for a few minutes.
7. Remove the bread from the pan and allow to cool on a wire rack for at least 10 minutes before slicing.

Nutrition per slice
Calories 221, fat 2.7 g, carbs 38.6 g,
sodium 227 mg, protein 4.8 g

Strawberry Oat Bread

Makes 1 loaf

Ingredients

<u>16 slice bread (2 pounds)</u>
1½ cups lukewarm milk
¼ cup unsalted butter, melted
¼ cup sugar
2 teaspoons table salt
1½ cups quick oats
3 cups white bread flour
2 teaspoons bread machine yeast
1 cup strawberries, sliced

<u>12 slice bread (1½ pounds)</u>
1⅛ cups lukewarm milk
3 tablespoons unsalted butter, melted
3 tablespoons sugar
1½ teaspoons table salt
1 cup quick oats
2¼ cups white bread flour
1½ teaspoons bread machine yeast
¾ cup strawberries, sliced

Directions

1. Choose the size of loaf you would like to make and measure your ingredients.
2. Add all of the ingredients except for the strawberries to the bread pan in the order listed above.
3. Place the pan in the bread machine and close the lid.
4. Turn on the bread maker. Select the White/Basic or Fruit/Nut (if your machine has this setting) setting, then the loaf size, and finally the crust color. Start the cycle.

5. When the machine signals to add ingredients, add the strawberries. (Some machines have a fruit/nut hopper where you can add the strawberries when you start the machine. The machine will automatically add them to the dough during the baking process.)
6. When the cycle is finished and the bread is baked, carefully remove the pan from the machine. Use a pot holder as the handle will be very hot. Let rest for a few minutes.
7. Remove the bread from the pan and allow to cool on a wire rack for at least 10 minutes before slicing.

Nutrition per slice
Calories 164, fat 3.8 g, carbs 26.7 g, sodium 314 mg, protein 4 g

Cinnamon Figs Bread

Makes 1 loaf

Ingredients

<u>16 slice bread (2 pounds)</u>
1½ cups lukewarm water
3 tablespoons unsalted butter, melted
¼ cup sugar
1 teaspoon table salt
½ teaspoon cinnamon, ground
1 teaspoon orange zest
Pinch ground nutmeg
2½ cups whole-wheat flour
1½ cups white bread flour
2 teaspoons bread machine yeast
1¼ cups chopped fresh plums or sliced figs

<u>12 slice bread (1½ pounds)</u>
1⅛ cups lukewarm water
2¼ tablespoons unsalted butter, melted
3 tablespoons sugar
¾ teaspoon table salt
⅓ teaspoon cinnamon, ground
¾ teaspoon orange zest
Pinch ground nutmeg
1⅞ cups whole-wheat flour
1⅛ cups white bread flour
1½ teaspoons bread machine yeast
1 cup chopped plums or sliced figs

Directions

1. Choose the size of loaf you would like to make and measure your ingredients.
2. Add all of the ingredients except for the plums to the bread pan in the order listed above.
3. Place the pan in the bread machine and close the lid.
4. Turn on the bread maker. Select the White/Basic or Fruit/Nut (if your machine has this setting) setting, then the loaf size, and finally the crust color. Start the cycle.
5. When the machine signals to add ingredients, add the plums. (Some machines have a fruit/nut hopper where you can add the plums when you start the machine. The machine will automatically add them to the dough during the baking process.)
6. When the cycle is finished and the bread is baked, carefully remove the pan from the machine. Use a pot holder as the handle will be very hot. Let rest for a few minutes.
7. Remove the bread from the pan and allow to cool on a wire rack for at least 10 minutes before slicing.

Nutrition per slice
Calories 136, fat 2.2 g, carbs 24.6 g, sodium 148 mg, protein 3.5 g

Cranberry Honey Bread

Makes 1 loaf

Ingredients

<u>16 slice bread (2 pounds)</u>
1¼ cups + 1 tablespoon lukewarm water
¼ cup unsalted butter, melted
3 tablespoons honey or molasses
4 cups white bread flour
½ cup cornmeal
2 teaspoons table salt
2½ teaspoons bread machine yeast
¾ cup cranberries, dried

<u>12 slice bread (1½ pounds)</u>
1 cup + 1 tablespoon lukewarm water
2 tablespoons unsalted butter, melted
3 tablespoons honey or molasses
3 cups white bread flour
⅓ cup cornmeal
1½ teaspoons table salt
2 teaspoons bread machine yeast
½ cup cranberries, dried

Directions

1. Choose the size of loaf you would like to make and measure your ingredients.
2. Add all of the ingredients except for the dried cranberries to the bread pan in the order listed above.
3. Place the pan in the bread machine and close the lid.
4. Turn on the bread maker. Select the White/Basic or Fruit/Nut (if your machine has this setting) setting, then the loaf size, and finally the crust color. Start the cycle.

5. When the machine signals to add ingredients, add the dried cranberries. (Some machines have a fruit/nut hopper where you can add the dried cranberries when you start the machine. The machine will automatically add them to the dough during the baking process.)
6. When the cycle is finished and the bread is baked, carefully remove the pan from the machine. Use a pot holder as the handle will be very hot. Let rest for a few minutes.
7. Remove the bread from the pan and allow to cool on a wire rack for at least 10 minutes before slicing.

Nutrition per slice
Calories 174, fat 2.6 g, carbs 33.6 g, sodium 310 mg, protein 4 g

Orange Bread

Makes 1 loaf

Ingredients

16 slice bread (2 pounds)
1¼ cups lukewarm milk
¼ cup orange juice
¼ cup sugar
1½ tablespoons unsalted butter, melted
1¼ teaspoons table salt
4 cups white bread flour
Zest of 1 orange
1¾ teaspoons bread machine yeast

12 slice bread (1½ pounds)
1 cup lukewarm milk
3 tablespoons orange juice
3 tablespoons sugar
1 tablespoon unsalted butter, melted
1 teaspoon table salt
3 cups white bread flour
Zest of 1 orange
1¼ teaspoons bread machine yeast

Directions
1. Choose the size of loaf you would like to make and measure your ingredients.
2. Add the ingredients to the bread pan in the order listed above.
3. Place the pan in the bread machine and close the lid.
4. Turn on the bread maker. Select the White/Basic setting, then the loaf size, and finally the crust color. Start the cycle.

5. When the cycle is finished and the bread is baked, carefully remove the pan from the machine. Use a pot holder as the handle will be very hot. Let rest for a few minutes.
6. Remove the bread from the pan and allow to cool on a wire rack for at least 10 minutes before slicing.

Nutrition per slice
Calories 153, fat 2.3 g, carbs 26.7 g,
sodium 243 mg, protein 3.8 g

Honey Banana Bread

Makes 1 loaf

Ingredients

16 slice bread (2 pounds)
⅔ cup lukewarm milk
1⅓ cups banana, mashed
1 egg, beaten
2 tablespoons unsalted butter, melted
¼ cup honey
1⅓ teaspoons pure vanilla extract
⅔ teaspoon table salt
1⅓ cups whole-wheat flour
1⅔ cups white bread flour
2 teaspoons bread machine yeast

12 slice bread (1½ pounds)
½ cup lukewarm milk
1 cup banana, mashed
1 egg, beaten
1½ tablespoons unsalted butter, melted
3 tablespoons honey
1 teaspoon pure vanilla extract
½ teaspoon table salt
1 cup whole-wheat flour
1¼ cups white bread flour
1½ teaspoons bread machine yeast

Directions

1. Choose the size of loaf you would like to make and measure your ingredients.
2. Add the ingredients to the bread pan in the order listed above.
3. Place the pan in the bread machine and close the lid.
4. Turn on the bread maker. Select the Sweet setting, then the loaf size, and finally the crust color. Start the cycle.
5. When the cycle is finished and the bread is baked, carefully remove the pan from the machine. Use a pot holder as the handle will be very hot. Let rest for a few minutes.
6. Remove the bread from the pan and allow to cool on a wire rack for at least 10 minutes before slicing.

Nutrition per slice

Calories 153, fat 3.4 g, carbs 27.1 g,
sodium 131 mg, protein 4.2 g

Garlic Olive Bread

Makes 1 loaf

Ingredients

<u>16 slice bread (2 pounds)</u>
1⅓ cups lukewarm milk
2 tablespoons unsalted butter, melted
1⅓ teaspoons garlic, minced
2 tablespoons sugar
1⅓ teaspoons table salt
4 cups white bread flour
1½ teaspoons bread machine yeast
½ cup black olives, chopped

<u>12 slice bread (1½ pounds)</u>
1 cup lukewarm milk
1½ tablespoons unsalted butter, melted
1 teaspoon garlic, minced
1½ tablespoons sugar
1 teaspoon table salt
3 cups white bread flour
1 teaspoon bread machine yeast
⅓ cup black olives, chopped

Directions
1. Choose the size of loaf you would like to make and measure your ingredients.
2. Add all of the ingredients except for the olives to the bread pan in the order listed above.
3. Place the pan in the bread machine and close the lid.
4. Turn on the bread maker. Select the White/Basic or Fruit/Nut (if your machine has this setting) setting, then the loaf size, and finally the crust color. Start the machine.

5. When the machine signals to add ingredients, add the olives. (Some machines have a fruit/nut hopper where you can add the olives when you start the machine. The machine will automatically add them to the dough during the baking process.)
6. When the cycle is finished and the bread is baked, carefully remove the pan from the machine. Use a pot holder as the handle will be very hot. Let rest for a few minutes.
7. Remove the bread from the pan and allow to cool on a wire rack for at least 10 minutes before slicing.

Nutrition per slice
Calories 143, fat 2.9 g, carbs 26.7 g, sodium 243 mg, protein 4.2 g

Cinnamon Pumpkin Bread

Makes 1 loaf

Ingredients

<u>16 slice bread (2 pounds)</u>
2 cups pumpkin puree
4 eggs, slightly beaten
½ cup unsalted butter, melted
1¼ cups sugar
½ teaspoon table salt
4 cups white bread flour
1 teaspoon cinnamon, ground
¾ teaspoon baking soda
½ teaspoon nutmeg, ground
½ teaspoon ginger, ground
Pinch ground cloves
2 teaspoons baking powder

<u>12 slice bread (1½ pounds)</u>
1½ cups pumpkin puree
3 eggs, slightly beaten
⅓ cup unsalted butter, melted
1 cup sugar
¼ teaspoon table salt
3 cups white bread flour
¾ teaspoon cinnamon, ground
½ teaspoon baking soda
¼ teaspoon nutmeg, ground
¼ teaspoon ginger, ground
Pinch ground cloves
1½ teaspoons baking powder

Directions

1. Choose the size of loaf you would like to make and measure your ingredients.
2. Add the ingredients to the bread pan in the order listed above.
3. Place the pan in the bread machine and close the lid.
4. Turn on the bread maker. Select the Quick/Rapid setting, then the loaf size, and finally the crust color. Start the cycle.
5. When the cycle is finished and the bread is baked, carefully remove the pan from the machine. Use a pot holder as the handle will be very hot. Let rest for a few minutes.
6. Remove the bread from the pan and allow to cool on a wire rack for at least 10 minutes before slicing.

Nutrition per slice
Calories 246, fat 6.7 g, carbs 37.6 g, sodium 146 mg, protein 5.2 g

SPICE AND NUT BREADS

Super Spice Bread

Makes 1 loaf

Ingredients
16 slice bread (2 pounds)
1⅓ cups lukewarm milk
2 eggs, at room temperature
2 tablespoons unsalted butter, melted
2⅔ tablespoons honey
1⅓ teaspoons table salt
4 cups white bread flour
1⅓ teaspoons ground cinnamon
⅔ teaspoon ground cardamom
⅔ teaspoon ground nutmeg
2¼ teaspoons bread machine yeast

12 slice bread (1½ pounds)
1 cup lukewarm milk
2 eggs, at room temperature
1½ tablespoons unsalted butter, melted
2 tablespoons honey
1 teaspoon table salt
3 cups white bread flour
1 teaspoon ground cinnamon
½ teaspoon ground cardamom
½ teaspoon ground nutmeg
2 teaspoons bread machine yeast

Directions

1. Choose the size of loaf you would like to make and measure your ingredients.
2. Add the ingredients to the bread pan in the order listed above.
3. Place the pan in the bread machine and close the lid.
4. Turn on the bread maker. Select the White/Basic setting, then the loaf size, and finally the crust color. Start the cycle.
5. When the cycle is finished and the bread is baked, carefully remove the pan from the machine. Use a pot holder as the handle will be very hot. Let rest for a few minutes.
6. Remove the bread from the pan and allow to cool on a wire rack for at least 10 minutes before slicing.

Nutrition per slice
Calories 163, fat 2.8 g, carbs 27.6 g, sodium 197 mg, protein 4.8 g

Almond Milk Bread

Makes 1 loaf

Ingredients

<u>16 slice bread (2 pounds)</u>
1 cup lukewarm milk
2 eggs, at room temperature
2⅔ tablespoons butter, melted and cooled
⅓ cup sugar
1 teaspoon table salt
2⅓ teaspoons lemon zest
4 cups white bread flour
2¼ teaspoons bread machine yeast
½ cup slivered almonds, chopped
½ cup golden raisins, chopped

<u>12 slice bread (1½ pounds)</u>
¾ cup lukewarm milk
2 eggs, at room temperature
2 tablespoons butter, melted and cooled
¼ cup sugar
1 teaspoon table salt
2 teaspoons lemon zest
3 cups white bread flour
2 teaspoons bread machine yeast
⅓ cup slivered almonds, chopped
⅓ cup golden raisins, chopped

Directions
1. Choose the size of loaf you would like to make and measure your ingredients.
2. Add all of the ingredients except for the raisins and almonds to the bread pan in the order listed above.
3. Place the pan in the bread machine and close the lid.
4. Turn on the bread maker. Select the White/Basic or Fruit/Nut (if your machine has this setting) setting, then the loaf size, and finally the crust color. Start the cycle.
5. When the machine signals to add ingredients, add the raisins and almonds. (Some machines have a fruit/nut hopper where you can add the raisins and almonds when you start the machine. The machine will automatically add them to the dough during the baking process.)
6. When the cycle is finished and the bread is baked, carefully remove the pan from the machine. Use a pot holder as the handle will be very hot. Let rest for a few minutes.
7. Remove the bread from the pan and allow to cool on a wire rack for at least 10 minutes before slicing.

Nutrition per slice
Calories 193, fat 4.6 g, carbs 29.4 g,
sodium 214 mg, protein 5.7 g

Cinnamon Milk Bread

Makes 1 loaf

Ingredients

<u>16 slice bread (2 pounds)</u>
1⅔ cups lukewarm milk
1 egg, at room temperature
⅓ cup unsalted butter, melted
⅔ cup sugar
⅔ teaspoon table salt
4 cups white bread flour
2 teaspoons ground cinnamon
2¼ teaspoons bread machine yeast

<u>12 slice bread (1½ pounds)</u>
1 cup lukewarm milk
1 egg, at room temperature
¼ cup unsalted butter, melted
½ cup sugar
½ teaspoon table salt
3 cups white bread flour
1½ teaspoons ground cinnamon
2 teaspoons bread machine yeast

Directions
1. Choose the size of loaf you would like to make and measure your ingredients.
2. Add the ingredients to the bread pan in the order listed above.
3. Place the pan in the bread machine and close the lid.
4. Turn on the bread maker. Select the White/Basic setting, then the loaf size, and finally the crust color. Start the cycle.

5. When the cycle is finished and the bread is baked, carefully remove the pan from the machine. Use a pot holder as the handle will be very hot. Let rest for a few minutes.
6. Remove the bread from the pan and allow to cool on a wire rack for at least 10 minutes before slicing.

Nutrition per slice
Calories 187, fat 5.1 g, carbs 33.4 g,
sodium 143 mg, protein 4.6 g

Hazelnut Honey Bread

Makes 1 loaf

Ingredients

<u>16 slice bread (2 pounds)</u>
1⅓ cups lukewarm milk
2 eggs, at room temperature
5 tablespoons unsalted butter, melted
¼ cup honey
1 teaspoon pure vanilla extract
1 teaspoon table salt
4 cups white bread flour
1 cup toasted hazelnuts, finely ground
2 teaspoons bread machine yeast

<u>12 slice bread (1½ pounds)</u>
1 cup lukewarm milk
1 egg, at room temperature
3¾ tablespoons unsalted butter, melted
3 tablespoons honey
¾ teaspoon pure vanilla extract
¾ teaspoon table salt
3 cups white bread flour
¾ cup toasted hazelnuts, finely ground
1½ teaspoons bread machine yeast

Directions

1. Choose the size of loaf you would like to make and measure your ingredients.
2. Add the ingredients to the bread pan in the order listed above.
3. Place the pan in the bread machine and close the lid.

4. Turn on the bread maker. Select the White/Basic setting, then the loaf size, and finally the crust color. Start the cycle.
5. When the cycle is finished and the bread is baked, carefully remove the pan from the machine. Use a pot holder as the handle will be very hot. Let rest for a few minutes.
6. Remove the bread from the pan and allow to cool on a wire rack for at least 10 minutes before slicing.

Nutrition per slice
Calories 211, fat 7.6 g, carbs 28.7 g,
sodium 153 mg, protein 4.3 g

Cardamom Honey Bread

Makes 1 loaf

Ingredients

<u>16 slice bread (2 pounds)</u>
1⅛ cups lukewarm milk
1 egg, at room temperature
2 teaspoons unsalted butter, melted
¼ cup honey
1⅓ teaspoons table salt
4 cups white bread flour
1⅓ teaspoons ground cardamom
1⅔ teaspoons bread machine yeast

<u>12 slice bread (1½ pounds)</u>
¾ cup lukewarm milk
1 egg, at room temperature
1½ teaspoons unsalted butter, melted
3 tablespoons honey
1 teaspoon table salt
3 cups white bread flour
1 teaspoon ground cardamom
1¼ teaspoons bread machine yeast

Directions

1. Choose the size of loaf you would like to make and measure your ingredients.
2. Add the ingredients to the bread pan in the order listed above.
3. Place the pan in the bread machine and close the lid.
4. Turn on the bread maker. Select the White/Basic setting, then the loaf size, and finally the crust color. Start the cycle.

5. When the cycle is finished and the bread is baked, carefully remove the pan from the machine. Use a pot holder as the handle will be very hot. Let rest for a few minutes.
6. Remove the bread from the pan and allow to cool on a wire rack for at least 10 minutes before slicing.

Nutrition per slice
Calories 148, fat 2.2 g, carbs 28.2 g,
sodium 212 mg, protein 4.8 g

Pistachio Cherry Bread

Makes 1 loaf

Ingredients

<u>16 slice bread (2 pounds)</u>
1⅛ cups lukewarm water
1 egg, at room temperature
¼ cup butter, softened
¼ cup packed dark brown sugar
1½ teaspoons table salt
3¾ cups white bread flour
½ teaspoon ground nutmeg
Dash allspice
2 teaspoons bread machine yeast
1 cup dried cherries
½ cup unsalted pistachios, chopped

<u>12 slice bread (1½ pounds)</u>
¾ cup lukewarm water
1 egg, at room temperature
3 tablespoons butter, softened
3 tablespoons packed dark brown sugar
1⅛ teaspoons table salt
2¾ cups white bread flour
½ teaspoon ground nutmeg
Dash allspice
1½ teaspoons bread machine yeast
¾ cup dried cherries
⅓ cup unsalted pistachios, chopped

Directions
1. Choose the size of loaf you would like to make and measure your ingredients.
2. Add all of the ingredients except for the pistachios and cherries to the bread pan in the order listed above.
3. Place the pan in the bread machine and close the lid.
4. Turn on the bread maker. Select the White/Basic or Fruit/Nut (if your machine has this setting) setting, then the loaf size, and finally the crust color. Start the cycle.
5. When the machine signals to add ingredients, add the pistachios and cherries. (Some machines have a fruit/nut hopper where you can add the pistachios and cherries when you start the machine. The machine will automatically add them to the dough during the baking process.)
6. When the cycle is finished and the bread is baked, carefully remove the pan from the machine. Use a pot holder as the handle will be very hot. Let rest for a few minutes.
7. Remove the bread from the pan and allow to cool on a wire rack for at least 10 minutes before slicing.

Nutrition per slice
Calories 196, fat 5.3 g, carbs 27.8 g,
sodium 237 mg, protein 4.4 g

Mix Seed Raisin Bread

Makes 1 loaf

Ingredients

16 slice bread (2 pounds)
1½ cups lukewarm milk
2 tablespoons unsalted butter, melted
2 tablespoons honey
1 teaspoon table salt
2½ cups white bread flour
¼ cup flaxseed
¼ cup sesame seeds
1½ cups whole-wheat flour
2¼ teaspoons bread machine yeast
½ cup raisins

12 slice bread (1½ pounds)
1⅛ cups lukewarm milk
1½ tablespoons unsalted butter, melted
1½ tablespoons honey
¾ teaspoon table salt
1¾ cups white bread flour
3 tablespoons flaxseed
3 tablespoons sesame seeds
1¼ cups whole-wheat flour
1¾ teaspoons bread machine yeast
⅓ cup raisins

Directions

1. Choose the size of loaf you would like to make and measure your ingredients.
2. Add the ingredients to the bread pan in the order listed above.
3. Place the pan in the bread machine and close the lid.
4. Turn on the bread maker. Select the White/Basic setting, then the loaf size, and finally the crust color. Start the cycle.
5. When the cycle is finished and the bread is baked, carefully remove the pan from the machine. Use a pot holder as the handle will be very hot. Let rest for a few minutes.
6. Remove the bread from the pan and allow to cool on a wire rack for at least 10 minutes before slicing.

Nutrition per slice
Calories 176, fat 4.1 g, carbs 28 g, sodium 166 mg, protein 5.2 g

Anise Honey Bread

Makes 1 loaf

Ingredients
<u>16 slice bread (2 pounds)</u>
1 cup + 1 tablespoon lukewarm water
1 egg, at room temperature
⅓ cup butter, melted and cooled
⅓ cup honey
⅔ teaspoon table salt
4 cups white bread flour
1⅓ teaspoons anise seed
1⅓ teaspoons lemon zest
2½ teaspoons bread machine yeast

<u>12 slice bread (1½ pounds)</u>
¾ cup lukewarm water
1 egg, at room temperature
¼ cup butter, melted and cooled
¼ cup honey
½ teaspoon table salt
3 cups white bread flour
1 teaspoon anise seed
1 teaspoon lemon zest
2 teaspoons bread machine yeast

Directions
1. Choose the size of loaf you would like to make and measure your ingredients.
2. Add the ingredients to the bread pan in the order listed above.
3. Place the pan in the bread machine and close the lid.

4. Turn on the bread maker. Select the White/Basic setting, then the loaf size, and finally the crust color. Start the cycle.
5. When the cycle is finished and the bread is baked, carefully remove the pan from the machine. Use a pot holder as the handle will be very hot. Let rest for a few minutes.
6. Remove the bread from the pan and allow to cool on a wire rack for at least 10 minutes before slicing.

Nutrition per slice
Calories 157, fat 4.8 g, carbs 29.6 g,
sodium 134 mg, protein 4.7 g

Basic Pecan Bread

Makes 1 loaf

Ingredients

<u>16 slice bread (2 pounds)</u>
1⅓ cups lukewarm milk
2⅔ tablespoons unsalted butter, melted
1 egg, at room temperature
2⅔ tablespoons sugar
1⅓ teaspoons table salt
4 cups white bread flour
2 teaspoons bread machine yeast
1⅓ cups chopped pecans, toasted

<u>12 slice bread (1½ pounds)</u>
1 cup lukewarm milk
2 tablespoons unsalted butter, melted
1 egg, at room temperature
2 tablespoons sugar
1 teaspoon table salt
3 cups white bread flour
1½ teaspoons bread machine yeast
1 cup chopped pecans, toasted

Directions

1. Choose the size of loaf you would like to make and measure your ingredients.
2. Add all of the ingredients except for the toasted pecans to the bread pan in the order listed above.
3. Place the pan in the bread machine and close the lid.
4. Turn on the bread maker. Select the White/Basic or Fruit/Nut (if your machine has this setting) setting, then the loaf size, and finally the crust color. Start the cycle.

5. When the machine signals to add ingredients, add the toasted pecans. (Some machines have a fruit/nut hopper where you can add the toasted pecans when you start the machine. The machine will automatically add them to the dough during the baking process.)
6. When the cycle is finished and the bread is baked, carefully remove the pan from the machine. Use a pot holder as the handle will be very hot. Let rest for a few minutes.
7. Remove the bread from the pan and allow to cool on a wire rack for at least 10 minutes before slicing.

Nutrition per slice
Calories 168, fat 4.8 g, carbs 25.6 g, sodium 217 mg, protein 5 g

VEGETABLE BREADS

Beetroot Bread

Makes 1 loaf

Ingredients

<u>16 slice bread (2 pounds)</u>
1 cup lukewarm water
1 cup grated raw beetroot
2 tablespoons unsalted butter, melted
2 tablespoons sugar
2 teaspoons table salt
4 cups white bread flour
1⅔ teaspoons bread machine yeast

<u>12 slice bread (1½ pounds)</u>
¾ cups lukewarm water
¾ cup grated raw beetroot
1½ tablespoons unsalted butter, melted
1½ tablespoons sugar
1¼ teaspoons table salt
3 cups white bread flour
1¼ teaspoons bread machine yeast

Directions
1. Choose the size of loaf you would like to make and measure your ingredients.
2. Add the ingredients to the bread pan in the order listed above.
3. Place the pan in the bread machine and close the lid.

4. Turn on the bread maker. Select the White/Basic setting, then the loaf size, and finally the crust color. Start the cycle.
5. When the cycle is finished and the bread is baked, carefully remove the pan from the machine. Use a pot holder as the handle will be very hot. Let rest for a few minutes.
6. Remove the bread from the pan and allow to cool on a wire rack for at least 10 minutes before slicing.

Nutrition per slice
Calories 143, fat 2.3 g, carbs 26.4 g, sodium 268 mg, protein 4 g

Sweet Potato Bread

Makes 1 loaf

Ingredients

<u>16 slice bread (2 pounds)</u>
⅝ cup lukewarm water
1 cup plain sweet potatoes, peeled and mashed
2 tablespoons unsalted butter, melted
⅓ cup dark brown sugar
1½ teaspoons table salt
4 cups bread flour
¼ teaspoon ground nutmeg
¼ teaspoon cinnamon
1 teaspoon vanilla extract
2 tablespoons dry milk powder
2 teaspoons bread machine yeast

<u>12 slice bread (1½ pounds)</u>
⅓ cup + 2 tablespoons lukewarm water
¾ cup plain sweet potatoes, peeled and mashed
1½ tablespoons unsalted butter, melted
¼ cup dark brown sugar
1 teaspoon table salt
3 cups bread flour
⅛ teaspoon ground nutmeg
⅛ teaspoon cinnamon
¾ teaspoon vanilla extract
1½ tablespoons dry milk powder
1½ teaspoons bread machine yeast

Directions

1. Choose the size of loaf you would like to make and measure your ingredients.
2. Add the ingredients to the bread pan in the order listed above.
3. Place the pan in the bread machine and close the lid.
4. Turn on the bread maker. Select the White/Basic setting, then the loaf size, and finally the crust color. Start the cycle.
5. When the cycle is finished, and the bread is baked, carefully remove the pan from the machine. Use a pot holder as the handle will be very hot. Let rest for a few minutes.
6. Remove the bread from the pan and allow to cool on a wire rack for at least 10 minutes before slicing.

Nutrition per slice
Calories 167, fat 2.2 g, carbs 28.4 g, sodium 227 mg, protein 5 g

Basil Tomato Bread

Makes 1 loaf

Ingredients
<u>16 slice bread (2 pounds)</u>
1 cup lukewarm tomato sauce
1 tablespoon olive oil
1 tablespoon sugar
1 teaspoon table salt
3 cups white bread flour
¼ cup grated Parmesan cheese
2 tablespoons dried basil
1 tablespoon dried oregano
2¼ teaspoons bread machine yeast

<u>12 slice bread (1½ pounds)</u>
¾ cup lukewarm tomato sauce
¾ tablespoon olive oil
¾ tablespoon sugar
¾ teaspoon table salt
2¼ cups white bread flour
1½ tablespoons dried basil
¾ tablespoon dried oregano
3 tablespoons grated Parmesan cheese
2 teaspoons bread machine yeast

Directions
1. Choose the size of loaf you would like to make and measure your ingredients.
2. Add the ingredients to the bread pan in the order listed above.
3. Place the pan in the bread machine and close the lid.

4. Turn on the bread maker. Select the White/Basic setting, then the loaf size, and finally the crust color. Start the cycle.
5. When the cycle is finished and the bread is baked, carefully remove the pan from the machine. Use a pot holder as the handle will be very hot. Let rest for a few minutes.
6. Remove the bread from the pan and allow to cool on a wire rack for at least 10 minutes before slicing.

Nutrition per slice
Calories 113, fat 2.2 g, carbs 21 g, sodium 247 mg, protein 4.2 g

Zucchini Spice Bread

Makes 1 loaf

Ingredients

<u>16 slice bread (2 pounds)</u>
2 eggs, at room temperature
⅔ cup unsalted butter, melted
⅔ teaspoon table salt
1 cup shredded zucchini
⅔ cup light brown sugar
3 tablespoons sugar
2 cups all-purpose flour
⅔ teaspoon baking powder
⅔ teaspoon baking soda
⅓ teaspoon ground allspice
1⅓ teaspoons ground cinnamon
⅔ cup chopped pecans

<u>12 slice bread (1½ pounds)</u>
2 eggs, at room temperature
½ cup unsalted butter, melted
½ teaspoon table salt
¾ cup shredded zucchini
½ cup light brown sugar
2 tablespoons sugar
1½ cups all-purpose flour
½ teaspoon baking powder
½ teaspoon baking soda
¼ teaspoon ground allspice
1 teaspoon ground cinnamon
½ cup chopped pecans

Directions

1. Choose the size of loaf you would like to make and measure your ingredients.
2. Add the ingredients to the bread pan in the order listed above.
3. Place the pan in the bread machine and close the lid.
4. Turn on the bread maker. Select the Quick/Rapid setting, then the loaf size, and finally the crust color. Start the cycle.
5. When the cycle is finished and the bread is baked, carefully remove the pan from the machine. Use a pot holder as the handle will be very hot. Let rest for a few minutes.
6. Remove the bread from the pan and allow to cool down on a wire rack for at least 10 minutes or more before slicing.

Nutrition per slice

Calories 167, fat 8.3 g, carbs 19.7 g, sodium 223 mg, protein 3.2 g

Potato Honey Bread

Makes 1 loaf

Ingredients

<u>16 slice bread (2 pounds)</u>
1 cup lukewarm water
⅔ cup finely mashed potatoes, at room temperature
1 egg, at room temperature
½ cup unsalted butter, melted
2⅔ tablespoons honey
1⅓ teaspoons table salt
4 cups white bread flour
2¼ teaspoons bread machine yeast

<u>12 slice bread (1½ pounds)</u>
¾ cup lukewarm water
½ cup finely mashed potatoes, at room temperature
1 egg, at room temperature
¼ cup unsalted butter, melted
2 tablespoons honey
1 teaspoon table salt
3 cups white bread flour
2 teaspoons bread machine yeast

Directions
1. Choose the size of loaf you would like to make and measure your ingredients.
2. Add the ingredients to the bread pan in the order listed above.
3. Place the pan in the bread machine and close the lid.
4. Turn on the bread maker. Select the White/Basic setting, then the loaf size, and finally the crust color. Start the cycle.

5. When the cycle is finished and the bread is baked, carefully remove the pan from the machine. Use a pot holder as the handle will be very hot. Let rest for a few minutes.
6. Remove the bread from the pan and allow to cool on a wire rack for at least 10 minutes before slicing.

Nutrition per slice
Calories 174, fat 4.8 g, carbs 28 g, sodium 262 mg, protein 4.3 g

Onion Chive Bread

Makes 1 loaf

Ingredients

<u>16 slice bread (2 pounds)</u>
1¼ cups lukewarm water
¼ cup unsalted butter, melted
2 tablespoons sugar
1½ teaspoons table salt
4¼ cups white bread flour
¼ cup dried minced onion
2 tablespoons fresh chives, chopped
2¼ teaspoons bread machine yeast

<u>12 slice bread (1½ pounds)</u>
1 cup lukewarm water
3 tablespoons unsalted butter, melted
1½ tablespoons sugar
1⅛ teaspoons table salt
3⅛ cups white bread flour
3 tablespoons dried minced onion
1½ tablespoons fresh chives, chopped
1⅔ teaspoons bread machine yeast

Directions
1. Choose the size of loaf you would like to make and measure your ingredients.
2. Add the ingredients to the bread pan in the order listed above.
3. Place the pan in the bread machine and close the lid.
4. Turn on the bread maker. Select the White/Basic setting, then the loaf size, and finally the crust color. Start the cycle.

5. When the cycle is finished and the bread is baked, carefully remove the pan from the machine. Use a pot holder as the handle will be very hot. Let rest for a few minutes.
6. Remove the bread from the pan and allow to cool on a wire rack for at least 10 minutes before slicing.

Nutrition per slice
Calories 147, fat 3 g, carbs 26.2 g, sodium 223 mg, protein 4.6 g

Honey Potato Flakes Bread

Makes 1 loaf

Ingredients

<u>16 slice bread (2 pounds)</u>
1⅔ cups lukewarm milk
2⅔ tablespoons unsalted butter, melted
4 teaspoons honey
2 teaspoons table salt
4 cups white bread flour
1½ teaspoons dried thyme
⅔ cup instant potato flakes
2½ teaspoons bread machine yeast

<u>12 slice bread (1½ pounds)</u>
1¼ cups lukewarm milk
2 tablespoons unsalted butter, melted
1 tablespoon honey
1½ teaspoons table salt
3 cups white bread flour
1 teaspoon dried thyme
½ cup instant potato flakes
2 teaspoons bread machine yeast

Directions
1. Choose the size of loaf you would like to make and measure your ingredients.
2. Add the ingredients to the bread pan in the order listed above.
3. Place the pan in the bread machine and close the lid.
4. Turn on the bread maker. Select the White/Basic setting, then the loaf size, and finally the crust color. Start the cycle.

5. When the cycle is finished and the bread is baked, carefully remove the pan from the machine. Use a pot holder as the handle will be very hot. Let rest for a few minutes.
6. Remove the bread from the pan and allow to cool on a wire rack for at least 10 minutes before slicing.

Nutrition per slice
Calories 157, fat 3.1 g, carbs 27.8 g,
sodium 294 mg, protein 4.8 g

Zucchini Lemon Bread

Makes 1 loaf

Ingredients

<u>16 slice bread (2 pounds)</u>
⅔ cup lukewarm milk
1 cup finely shredded zucchini
⅓ teaspoon lemon juice, at room temperature
4 teaspoons olive oil
4 teaspoons sugar
1⅓ teaspoons table salt
1 cup whole-wheat flour
2 cups white bread flour
1 cup quick oats
2¼ teaspoons bread machine yeast

<u>12 slice bread (1½ pounds)</u>
½ cup lukewarm milk
¾ cup finely shredded zucchini
¼ teaspoon lemon juice, at room temperature
1 tablespoon olive oil
1 tablespoon sugar
1 teaspoon table salt
¾ cup whole-wheat flour
1½ cups white bread flour
¾ cup quick oats
2¼ teaspoons bread machine yeast

Directions
1. Choose the size of loaf you would like to make and measure your ingredients.
2. Add the ingredients to the bread pan in the order listed above.

3. Place the pan in the bread machine and close the lid.
4. Turn on the bread maker. Select the White/Basic setting, then the loaf size, and finally the crust color. Start the cycle.
5. When the cycle is finished and the bread is baked, carefully remove the pan from the machine. Use a pot holder as the handle will be very hot. Let rest for a few minutes.
6. Remove the bread from the pan and allow to cool on a wire rack for at least 10 minutes before slicing.

Nutrition per slice
Calories 127, fat 2 g, carbs 23.4 g, sodium 194 mg, protein 4.1 g

CHEESE AND HERB BREADS

Romano Oregano Bread

Makes 1 loaf

Ingredients
<u>16 slice bread (2 pounds)</u>
1⅓ cups lukewarm water
¼ cup sugar
2 tablespoons olive oil
1⅓ teaspoons table salt
1⅓ tablespoons dried leaf oregano
⅔ cup cheese (Romano or Parmesan), freshly grated
4 cups white bread flour
2½–3 teaspoons bread machine yeast

<u>12 slice bread (1½ pounds)</u>
1 cup lukewarm water
3 tablespoons sugar
1½ tablespoons olive oil
1 teaspoon table salt
1 tablespoon dried leaf oregano
½ cup cheese (Romano or Parmesan), freshly grated
3 cups white bread flour
2 teaspoons bread machine yeast

Directions
1. Choose the size of loaf you would like to make and measure your ingredients.
2. Add the ingredients to the bread pan in the order listed above.
3. Place the pan in the bread machine and close the lid.

4. Turn on the bread maker. Select the White/Basic setting, then the loaf size, and finally the crust color. Start the cycle.
5. When the cycle is finished and the bread is baked, carefully remove the pan from the machine. Use a pot holder as the handle will be very hot. Let rest for a few minutes.
6. Remove the bread from the pan and allow to cool down on a wire rack for at least 10 minutes or more before slicing.

Nutrition per slice
Calories 207, fat 6.2 g, carbs 27 g, sodium 267 mg, protein 9.3 g

Mexican Style Jalapeno Cheese Bread

Makes 1 loaf

Ingredients
16 slice bread (2 pounds)
1 small jalapeno pepper, seeded and minced
1 cup lukewarm water
3 tablespoons nonfat dry milk powder
1½ tablespoons unsalted butter, melted
1½ tablespoons sugar
1½ teaspoons table salt
¼ cup finely shredded cheese (Mexican blend or Monterrey Jack)
3 cups white bread flour
2 teaspoons bread machine yeast

12 slice bread (1½ pounds)
1 small jalapeno pepper, seeded and minced
¾ cup lukewarm water
2 tablespoons nonfat dry milk powder
1 tablespoons unsalted butter, melted
1 tablespoons sugar
1 teaspoon table salt
3 tablespoons finely shredded cheese (Mexican blend or Monterrey Jack)
2 cups white bread flour
1½ teaspoons bread machine yeast

Directions
1. Choose the size of loaf you would like to make and measure your ingredients.
2. Add the ingredients to the bread pan in the order listed above.

3. Place the pan in the bread machine and close the lid.
4. Turn on the bread maker. Select the White/Basic setting, then the loaf size, and finally the crust color. Start the cycle.
5. When the cycle is finished and the bread is baked, carefully remove the pan from the machine. Use a pot holder as the handle will be very hot. Let rest for a few minutes.
6. Remove the bread from the pan and allow to cool on a wire rack for at least 10 minutes before slicing.

Nutrition per slice
Calories 220, fat 9.4 g, carbs 18.6 g, sodium 206 mg, protein 9 g

Jalapeno Cheddar Bread

Makes 1 loaf

Ingredients
<u>16 slice bread (2 pounds)</u>
1⅓ cups lukewarm buttermilk
⅓ cup unsalted butter, melted
2 eggs, at room temperature
⅔ teaspoon table salt
1 jalapeno pepper, chopped
⅔ cup Cheddar cheese, shredded
⅓ cup sugar
2 cups all-purpose flour
1⅓ cups cornmeal
1½ tablespoons baking powder

<u>12 slice bread (1½ pounds)</u>
1 cup lukewarm buttermilk
¼ cup unsalted butter, melted
2 eggs, at room temperature
½ teaspoon table salt
1 jalapeno pepper, chopped
½ cup Cheddar cheese, shredded
¼ cup sugar
1⅓ cups all-purpose flour
1 cup cornmeal
1 tablespoon baking powder

Directions
1. Choose the size of loaf you would like to make and measure your ingredients.
2. Add the ingredients to the bread pan in the order listed above.

3. Place the pan in the bread machine and close the lid.
4. Turn on the bread maker. Select the Rapid/Quick setting, then the loaf size, and finally the crust color. Start the cycle.
5. When the cycle is finished and the bread is baked, carefully remove the pan from the machine. Use a pot holder as the handle will be very hot. Let rest for a few minutes.
6. Remove the bread from the pan and allow to cool on a wire rack for at least 10 minutes before slicing.

Nutrition per slice
Calories 173, fat 6.2 g, carbs 24.3 g, sodium 187 mg, protein 4.8 g

Parsley Garlic Bread

Makes 1 loaf

Ingredients

<u>16 slice bread (2 pounds)</u>
1⅓ cups lukewarm milk
2 tablespoons unsalted butter, melted
4 teaspoons sugar
2 teaspoons table salt
2⅔ teaspoons garlic powder
2⅔ teaspoons fresh parsley, chopped
4 cups white bread flour
2¼ teaspoons bread machine yeast

<u>12 slice bread (1½ pounds)</u>
1 cup lukewarm milk
1½ tablespoons unsalted butter, melted
1 tablespoon sugar
1½ teaspoons table salt
2 teaspoons garlic powder
2 teaspoons fresh parsley, chopped
3 cups white bread flour
1¾ teaspoons bread machine yeast

Directions

1. Choose the size of loaf you would like to make and measure your ingredients.
2. Add the ingredients to the bread pan in the order listed above.
3. Place the pan in the bread machine and close the lid.
4. Turn on the bread maker. Select the White/Basic setting, then the loaf size, and finally the crust color. Start the cycle.

5. When the cycle is finished and the bread is baked, carefully remove the pan from the machine. Use a pot holder as the handle will be very hot. Let rest for a few minutes.
6. Remove the bread from the pan and allow to cool on a wire rack for at least 10 minutes before slicing.

Nutrition per slice
Calories 143, fat 2.2 g, carbs 24.6 g,
sodium 317 mg, protein 4.3 g

Cheddar Bacon Bread

Makes 1 loaf

Ingredients

<u>16 slice bread (2 pounds)</u>
⅔ cup lukewarm milk
2 teaspoons unsalted butter, melted
2 tablespoons honey
2 teaspoons table salt
⅔ cup green chilies, chopped
⅔ cup grated Cheddar cheese
⅔ cup cooked bacon, chopped
4 cups white bread flour
2½ teaspoons bread machine yeast

<u>12 slice bread (1½ pounds)</u>
½ cup lukewarm milk
1½ teaspoons unsalted butter, melted
1½ tablespoons honey
1½ teaspoons table salt
½ cup green chilies, chopped
½ cup grated Cheddar cheese
½ cup cooked bacon, chopped
3 cups white bread flour
2 teaspoons bread machine yeast

Directions
1. Choose the size of loaf you would like to make and measure your ingredients.
2. Add the ingredients to the bread pan in the order listed above.
3. Place the pan in the bread machine and close the lid.

4. Turn on the bread maker. Select the White/Basic setting, then the loaf size, and finally the crust color. Start the cycle.
5. When the cycle is finished and the bread is baked, carefully remove the pan from the machine. Use a pot holder as the handle will be very hot. Let rest for a few minutes.
6. Remove the bread from the pan and allow to cool on a wire rack for at least 10 minutes before slicing.

Nutrition per slice
Calories 172, fat 3.8 g, carbs 36.4 g,
sodium 234 mg, protein 6.2 g

Mixed Herb Cheese Bread

Makes 1 loaf

Ingredients

16 slice bread (2 pounds)
1⅓ cups lukewarm water
2 tablespoons olive oil
1 teaspoon table salt
1 tablespoon sugar
2 cloves garlic, crushed
3 tablespoons mixed fresh herbs (basil, chives, oregano, rosemary etc.)
¼ cup Parmesan cheese, grated
4 cups white bread flour
2¼ teaspoons bread machine yeast

12 slice bread (1½ pounds)
1 cup lukewarm water
1½ tablespoons olive oil
¾ teaspoon table salt
¾ tablespoon sugar
2 cloves garlic, crushed
2 tablespoons mixed fresh herbs (basil, chives, oregano, rosemary etc.)
3 tablespoons Parmesan cheese, grated
3 cups white bread flour
1⅔ teaspoons bread machine yeast

Directions

1. Choose the size of loaf you would like to make and measure your ingredients.
2. Add the ingredients to the bread pan in the order listed above.
3. Place the pan in the bread machine and close the lid.
4. Turn on the bread maker. Select the White/Basic setting, then the loaf size, and finally the crust color. Start the cycle.
5. When the cycle is finished and the bread is baked, carefully remove the pan from the machine. Use a pot holder as the handle will be very hot. Let rest for a few minutes.
6. Remove the bread from the pan and allow to cool on a wire rack for at least 10 minutes before slicing.

Nutrition per slice

Calories 147, fat 3.2 g, carbs 25.3 g, sodium 37 mg, protein 5.1 g

Basil Cheese Bread

Makes 1 loaf

Ingredients

16 slice bread (2 pounds)
1⅓ cups lukewarm milk
4 teaspoons unsalted butter, melted
4 teaspoons sugar
1¼ teaspoons dried basil
1 teaspoon table salt
1 cup sharp Cheddar cheese, shredded
4 cups white bread flour
2 teaspoons bread machine yeast

12 slice bread (1½ pounds)
1 cup lukewarm milk
1 tablespoon unsalted butter, melted
1 tablespoon sugar
1 teaspoon dried basil
¾ teaspoon table salt
¾ cup sharp Cheddar cheese, shredded
3 cups white bread flour
1½ teaspoons bread machine yeast

Directions
1. Choose the size of loaf you would like to make and measure your ingredients.
2. Add the ingredients to the bread pan in the order listed above.
3. Place the pan in the bread machine and close the lid.
4. Turn on the bread maker. Select the White/Basic setting, then the loaf size, and finally the crust color. Start the cycle.

5. When the cycle is finished and the bread is baked, carefully remove the pan from the machine. Use a pot holder as the handle will be very hot. Let rest for a few minutes.
6. Remove the bread from the pan and allow to cool on a wire rack for at least 10 minutes before slicing.

Nutrition per slice
Calories 167, fat 3.8 g, carbs 25.7 g,
sodium 209 mg, protein 5.7 g

American Cheese Beer Bread

Makes 1 loaf

Ingredients
<u>16 slice bread (2 pounds)</u>
1⅔ cups warm beer
1½ tablespoons sugar
2 teaspoons table salt
1½ tablespoons unsalted butter, melted
¾ cup American cheese, shredded
¾ cup Monterrey Jack cheese, shredded
4 cups white bread flour
2 teaspoons bread machine yeast

<u>12 slice bread (1½ pounds)</u>
1¼ cups warm beer
1 tablespoon sugar
1½ teaspoons table salt
1 tablespoon unsalted butter, melted
½ cup American cheese, shredded
½ cup Monterrey Jack cheese, shredded
3 cups white bread flour
1½ teaspoons bread machine yeast

Directions
1. Choose the size of loaf you would like to make and measure your ingredients.
2. Add the ingredients to the bread pan in the order listed above.
3. Place the pan in the bread machine and close the lid.
4. Turn on the bread maker. Select the White/Basic setting, then the loaf size, and finally the crust color. Start the cycle.

5. When the cycle is finished and the bread is baked, carefully remove the pan from the machine. Use a pot holder as the handle will be very hot. Let rest for a few minutes.
6. Remove the bread from the pan and allow to cool on a wire rack for at least 10 minutes before slicing.

Nutrition per slice
Calories 173, fat 5.3 g, carbs 26.1 g, sodium 118 mg, protein 6.2 g

Swiss Olive Bread

Makes 1 loaf

Ingredients

<u>16 slice bread (2 pounds)</u>
1⅓ cups lukewarm milk
2 tablespoons unsalted butter, melted
1⅓ teaspoons minced garlic
2 tablespoons sugar
1⅓ teaspoons table salt
1 cup Swiss cheese, shredded
4 cups white bread flour
1½ teaspoons bread machine yeast
½ cup chopped black olives

<u>12 slice bread (1½ pounds)</u>
1 cup lukewarm milk
1½ tablespoons unsalted butter, melted
1 teaspoon minced garlic
1½ tablespoons sugar
1 teaspoon table salt
¾ cup Swiss cheese, shredded
3 cups white bread flour
1 teaspoon bread machine yeast
⅓ cup chopped black olives

Directions
1. Choose the size of loaf you would like to make and measure your ingredients.
2. Add all of the ingredients except for the olives to the bread pan in the order listed above.
3. Place the pan in the bread machine and close the lid.

4. Turn on the bread maker. Select the White/Basic or Fruit/Nut (if your machine has this setting) setting, then the loaf size, and finally the crust color. Start the cycle.
5. When the machine signals to add ingredients, add the olives. (Some machines have a fruit/nut hopper where you can add the olives when you start the machine. The machine will automatically add them to the dough during the baking process.)
6. When the cycle is finished and the bread is baked, carefully remove the pan from the machine. Use a pot holder as the handle will be very hot. Let rest for a few minutes.
7. Remove the bread from the pan and allow to cool on a wire rack for at least 10 minutes before slicing.

Nutrition per slice
Calories 147, fat 4.8 g, carbs 26.7 g, sodium 263 mg, protein 5.8 g

Parmesan Cheddar Bread

Makes 1 loaf

Ingredients

16 slice bread (2 pounds)
1⅔ cups lukewarm milk
4 teaspoons unsalted butter, melted
2⅔ tablespoons sugar
1⅓ teaspoons table salt
⅔ teaspoon freshly ground black pepper
Pinch cayenne pepper
2 cups shredded aged sharp Cheddar cheese
⅔ cup shredded Parmesan cheese
4 cups white bread flour
1⅔ teaspoons bread machine yeast

12 slice bread (1½ pounds)
1¼ cups lukewarm milk
1 tablespoon unsalted butter, melted
2 tablespoons sugar
1 teaspoon table salt
½ teaspoon freshly ground black pepper
Pinch cayenne pepper
1½ cups shredded aged sharp Cheddar cheese
½ cup shredded or grated Parmesan cheese
3 cups white bread flour
1¼ teaspoons bread machine yeast

Directions
1. Choose the size of loaf you would like to make and measure your ingredients.
2. Add the ingredients to the bread pan in the order listed above.

3. Place the pan in the bread machine and close the lid.
4. Turn on the bread maker. Select the White/Basic setting, then the loaf size, and finally the crust color. Start the cycle.
5. When the cycle is finished and the bread is baked, carefully remove the pan from the machine. Use a pot holder as the handle will be very hot. Let rest for a few minutes.
6. Remove the bread from the pan and allow to cool on a wire rack for at least 10 minutes before slicing.

Nutrition per slice
Calories 173, fat 4.3 g, carbs 27.4 g,
sodium 326 mg, protein 8.7 g

Honey Goat Cheese Bread

Makes 1 loaf

Ingredients

<u>16 slice bread (2 pounds)</u>
1⅓ cups lukewarm milk
2 tablespoons honey
1⅓ teaspoons table salt
1⅓ teaspoons ground black pepper
5 tablespoons goat cheese, shredded or crumbled
4 cups white bread flour
2 teaspoons bread machine yeast

<u>12 slice bread (1½ pounds)</u>
1 cup lukewarm milk
1½ tablespoons honey
1 teaspoon table salt
1 teaspoon freshly cracked black pepper
¼ cup goat cheese, shredded or crumbled
3 cups white bread flour
1½ teaspoons bread machine yeast

Directions

1. Choose the size of loaf you would like to make and measure your ingredients.
2. Add the ingredients to the bread pan in the order listed above.
3. Place the pan in the bread machine and close the lid.
4. Turn on the bread maker. Select the White/Basic setting, then the loaf size, and finally the crust color. Start the cycle.

5. When the cycle is finished and the bread is baked, carefully remove the pan from the machine. Use a pot holder as the handle will be very hot. Let rest for a few minutes.
6. Remove the bread from the pan and allow to cool on a wire rack for at least 10 minutes before slicing.

Nutrition per slice
Calories 144, fat 2.3 g, carbs 26.4 g,
sodium 223 mg, protein 4.9 g

Sweet Breads

Apple Honey Bread

Makes 1 loaf

Ingredients

<u>16 slice bread (2 pounds)</u>
7 tablespoons tablespoon lukewarm milk
¼ cup apple cider, at room temperature
¼ cup sugar
2⅔ tablespoons unsalted butter, melted
2 tablespoons honey
¼ teaspoon table salt
4 cups white bread flour
1⅔ teaspoons bread machine yeast
1 apple, peeled, cored, and finely diced

<u>12 slice bread (1½ pounds)</u>
5 tablespoons lukewarm milk
3 tablespoons apple cider, at room temperature
3 tablespoons sugar
2 tablespoons unsalted butter, melted
1½ tablespoons honey
¼ teaspoon table salt
3 cups white bread flour
1¼ teaspoons bread machine yeast
1 apple, peeled, cored, and finely diced

Directions

1. Choose the size of loaf you would like to make and measure your ingredients.
2. Add all of the ingredients except for the apples to the bread pan in the order listed above.
3. Place the pan in the bread machine and close the lid.
4. Turn on the bread maker. Select the White/Basic or Fruit/Nut (if your machine has this setting) setting, then the loaf size, and finally the crust color. Start the cycle.
5. When the machine signals to add ingredients, add the apples. (Some machines have a fruit/nut hopper where you can add the apples when you start the machine. The machine will automatically add them to the dough during the baking process.)
6. When the cycle is finished and the bread is baked, carefully remove the pan from the machine. Use a pot holder as the handle will be very hot. Let rest for a few minutes.
7. Remove the bread from the pan and allow to cool on a wire rack for at least 10 minutes before slicing.

Nutrition per slice
Calories 156, fat 3 g, carbs 28.4 g, sodium 82 mg, protein 4.3 g

White Chocolate Bread

Makes 1 loaf

Ingredients

<u>16 slice bread (2 pounds)</u>
1⅓ cups lukewarm milk
1 egg, at room temperature
2⅔ tablespoons unsalted butter, melted
2 teaspoons pure vanilla extract
¼ cup light brown sugar
2 tablespoons cocoa powder, unsweetened
1 teaspoon table salt
4 cups white bread flour
1⅔ teaspoons bread machine yeast
½ cup semisweet chocolate chips
½ cup white chocolate chips

<u>12 slice bread (1½ pounds)</u>
1 cup lukewarm milk
1 egg, at room temperature
2 tablespoons unsalted butter, melted
1½ teaspoons pure vanilla extract
3 tablespoons light brown sugar
4 teaspoons cocoa powder, unsweetened
¾ teaspoon table salt
3 cups white bread flour
1¼ teaspoons bread machine yeast
⅓ cup semisweet chocolate chips
⅓ cup white chocolate chips

Directions

1. Choose the size of loaf you would like to make and measure your ingredients.
2. Take the bread pan; add the ingredients except both the chocolate chips to the bread pan in the order listed above.
3. Place the pan in the bread machine and close the lid.
4. Turn on the bread maker. Select the White/Basic or Fruit/Nut (if your machine has this setting) setting, then the loaf size, and finally the crust color. Start the cycle.
5. When the machine signals to add ingredients, add both the chocolate chips. (Some machines have a fruit/nut hopper where you can add both the chocolate chips when you start the machine. The machine will automatically add them to the dough during the baking process.)
6. When the cycle is finished and the bread is baked, carefully remove the pan from the machine. Use a pot holder as the handle will be very hot. Let rest for a few minutes.
7. Remove the bread from the pan and allow to cool on a wire rack for at least 10 minutes before slicing.

Nutrition per slice
Calories 238, fat 6.8 g, carbs 34.2 g, sodium 211 mg, protein 4.9 g

Ginger Spiced Bread

Makes 1 loaf

Ingredients

<u>16 slice bread (2 pounds)</u>
1⅓ cups lukewarm butter milk
1 egg, at room temperature
⅓ cup dark molasses
4 teaspoons unsalted butter, melted
¼ cup sugar
2 teaspoons table salt
4¼ cups white bread flour
2 teaspoons ground ginger
1¼ teaspoons ground cinnamon
⅔ teaspoon ground nutmeg
⅓ teaspoon ground cloves
2¼ teaspoons bread machine yeast

<u>12 slice bread (1½ pounds)</u>
1 cup lukewarm buttermilk
1 egg, at room temperature
¼ cup dark molasses
1 tablespoon unsalted butter, melted
3 tablespoons sugar
1½ teaspoons table salt
3½ cups white bread flour
1 teaspoon ground cinnamon
½ teaspoon ground nutmeg
¼ teaspoon ground cloves
1½ teaspoons ground ginger
2 teaspoons bread machine yeast

Directions

1. Choose the size of loaf you would like to make and measure your ingredients.
2. Add the ingredients to the bread pan in the order listed above.
3. Place the pan in the bread machine and close the lid.
4. Turn on the bread maker. Select the Sweet setting, then the loaf size, and finally the crust color. Start the cycle.
5. When the cycle is finished and the bread is baked, carefully remove the pan from the machine. Use a pot holder as the handle will be very hot. Let rest for a few minutes.
6. Remove the bread from the pan and allow to cool on a wire rack for at least 10 minutes before slicing.

Nutrition per slice

Calories 187, fat 2.3 g, carbs 36.7 g, sodium 312 mg, protein 4.6 g

Sweet Applesauce Bread

Makes 1 loaf

Ingredients

<u>16 slice bread (2 pounds)</u>
1 cup lukewarm milk
⅓ cup unsweetened applesauce, at room temperature
4 teaspoons unsalted butter, melted
4 teaspoons sugar
1⅓ teaspoons table salt
⅓ cup quick oats
3 cups white bread flour
¾ teaspoon ground cinnamon
Pinch ground nutmeg
2¼ teaspoons bread machine yeast

<u>12 slice bread (1½ pounds)</u>
⅔ cup lukewarm milk
¼ cup unsweetened applesauce, at room temperature
1 tablespoon unsalted butter, melted
1 tablespoon sugar
1 teaspoon table salt
¼ cup quick oats
2¼ cups white bread flour
½ teaspoon ground cinnamon
Pinch ground nutmeg
2¼ teaspoons bread machine yeast

Directions
1. Choose the size of loaf you would like to make and measure your ingredients.
2. Add the ingredients to the bread pan in the order listed above.

3. Place the pan in the bread machine and close the lid.
4. Turn on the bread maker. Select the White/Basic setting, then the loaf size, and finally the crust color. Start the cycle.
5. When the cycle is finished and the bread is baked, carefully remove the pan from the machine. Use a pot holder as the handle will be very hot. Let rest for a few minutes.
6. Remove the bread from the pan and allow to cool on a wire rack for at least 10 minutes before slicing.

Nutrition per slice
Calories 124, fat 2.4 g, carbs 23.1 g,
sodium 217 mg, protein 3.3 g

Milk Sweet Bread

Makes 1 loaf

Ingredients

16 slice bread (2 pounds)
1⅓ cups lukewarm milk
1 egg, at room temperature
2⅔ tablespoons butter, softened
⅔ cup sugar
1⅓ teaspoons table salt
4 cups white bread flour
2¼ teaspoons bread machine yeast

12 slice bread (1½ pounds)
1 cup lukewarm milk
1 egg, at room temperature
2 tablespoons butter, softened
½ cup sugar
1 teaspoon table salt
3 cups white bread flour
2¼ teaspoons bread machine yeast

Directions
1. Choose the size of loaf you would like to make and measure your ingredients.
2. Add the ingredients to the bread pan in the order listed above.
3. Place the pan in the bread machine and close the lid.
4. Turn on the bread maker. Select the Sweet setting, then the loaf size, and finally the crust color. Start the cycle.

5. When the cycle is finished and the bread is baked, carefully remove the pan from the machine. Use a pot holder as the handle will be very hot. Let rest for a few minutes.
6. Remove the bread from the pan and allow to cool on a wire rack for at least 10 minutes before slicing.

Nutrition per slice
Calories 178, fat 3.2 g, carbs 32.6 g,
sodium 227 mg, protein 4.8 g

Allspice Currant Bread

Makes 1 loaf

Ingredients

<u>16 slice bread (2 pounds)</u>
1½ cups lukewarm water
2 tablespoons unsalted butter, melted
¼ cup sugar
¼ cup skim milk powder
2 teaspoons table salt
4 cups white bread flour
1½ teaspoons dried lemon zest
¾ teaspoon ground allspice
¼ teaspoon ground nutmeg
2½ teaspoons bread machine yeast
1 cup dried currants

<u>12 slice bread (1½ pounds)</u>
1⅛ cups lukewarm water
1½ tablespoons unsalted butter, melted
3 tablespoons sugar
3 tablespoons skim milk powder
1½ teaspoons table salt
3 cups white bread flour
1 teaspoon dried lemon zest
½ teaspoon ground allspice
¼ teaspoon ground nutmeg
2½ teaspoons bread machine yeast
¾ cup dried currants

Directions

1. Choose the size of loaf you would like to make and measure your ingredients.
2. Add all of the ingredients except for the dried currants to the bread pan in the order listed above.
3. Place the pan in the bread machine and close the lid.
4. Turn on the bread maker. Select the White/Basic or Fruit/Nut (if your machine has this setting) setting, then the loaf size, and finally the crust color. Start the cycle.
5. When the machine signals to add ingredients, add the dried currants. (Some machines have a fruit/nut hopper where you can add the dried currants when you start the machine. The machine will automatically add them to the dough during the baking process.)
6. When the cycle is finished and the bread is baked, carefully remove the pan from the machine. Use a pot holder as the handle will be very hot. Let rest for a few minutes.
7. Remove the bread from the pan and allow to cool on a wire rack for at least 10 minutes before slicing.

Nutrition per slice

Calories 168, fat 2.5 g, carbs 32.3 g, sodium 306 mg, protein 4.8 g

Buttermilk Pecan Bread

Makes 1 loaf

Ingredients

<u>16 slice bread (2 pounds)</u>
1 cup buttermilk, at room temperature
1 cup butter, at room temperature
1⅓ tablespoons instant coffee granules
3 eggs, at room temperature
1 cup sugar
3 cups all-purpose flour
⅔ tablespoon baking powder
⅔ teaspoon table salt
1⅓ cups chopped pecans

<u>12 slice bread (1½ pounds)</u>
¾ cup buttermilk, at room temperature
¾ cup butter, at room temperature
1 tablespoon instant coffee granules
3 eggs, at room temperature
¾ cup sugar
2 cups all-purpose flour
½ tablespoon baking powder
½ teaspoon table salt
1 cup chopped pecans

Directions
1. Choose the size of loaf you would like to make and measure your ingredients.
2. Add the ingredients to the bread pan in the order listed above.
3. Place the pan in the bread machine and close the lid.

4. Turn on the bread maker. Select the Quick/Rapid setting, then the loaf size, and finally the crust color. Start the cycle.
5. When the cycle is finished and the bread is baked, carefully remove the pan from the machine. Use a pot holder as the handle will be very hot. Let rest for a few minutes.
6. Remove the bread from the pan and allow to cool on a wire rack for at least 10 minutes before slicing.

Nutrition per slice
Calories 262, fat 14.3 g, carbs 26.4 g,
sodium 217 mg, protein 4.7 g

Cashew Butter/Peanut Butter Bread

Makes 1 loaf

Ingredients

16 slice bread (2 pounds)
1⅓ cups peanut butter or cashew butter
1⅓ cups lukewarm milk
⅔ cup packed light brown sugar
⅓ cup sugar
⅓ cup butter, at room temperature
1 egg, at room temperature
3 teaspoons pure vanilla extract
3 cups all-purpose flour
1⅓ tablespoons baking powder
¾ teaspoon table salt

12 slice bread (1½ pounds)
1 cup peanut butter or cashew butter
1 cup lukewarm milk
½ cup packed light brown sugar
¼ cup sugar
¼ cup butter, at room temperature
1 egg, at room temperature
2 teaspoons pure vanilla extract
2 cups all-purpose flour
1 tablespoon baking powder
½ teaspoon table salt

Directions
1. Choose the size of loaf you would like to make and measure your ingredients.
2. Add the ingredients to the bread pan in the order listed above.

3. Place the pan in the bread machine and close the lid.
4. Turn on the bread maker. Select the Quick/Rapid setting, then the loaf size, and finally the crust color. Start the cycle.
5. When the cycle is finished and the bread is baked, carefully remove the pan from the machine. Use a pot holder as the handle will be very hot. Let rest for a few minutes.
6. Remove the bread from the pan and allow to cool down on a wire rack for at least 10 minutes or more before slicing.

Nutrition per slice
Calories 284, fat 13.6 g, carbs 31.8 g,
sodium 236 mg, protein 8.5 g

Delicious Sour Cream Bread

Makes 1 loaf

Ingredients

<u>16 slice bread (2 pounds)</u>
¾ cup lukewarm water
¾ cup sour cream, at room temperature
3 tablespoons butter, at room temperature
1½ tablespoons maple syrup
1 teaspoon table salt
3¾ cups white bread flour
2¼ teaspoons bread machine yeast

<u>12 slice bread (1½ pounds)</u>
½ cup + 1 tablespoon lukewarm water
½ cup + 1 tablespoon sour cream, at room temperature
2¼ tablespoons butter, at room temperature
1 tablespoon maple syrup
¾ teaspoon table salt
2¾ cups white bread flour
1⅔ teaspoons bread machine yeast

Directions
1. Choose the size of loaf you would like to make and measure your ingredients.
2. Add the ingredients to the bread pan in the order listed above.
3. Place the pan in the bread machine and close the lid.
4. Turn on the bread maker. Select the White/Basic setting, then the loaf size, and finally the crust color. Start the cycle.

5. When the cycle is finished and the bread is baked, carefully remove the pan from the machine. Use a pot holder as the handle will be very hot. Let rest for a few minutes.
6. Remove the bread from the pan and allow to cool down on a wire rack for at least 10 minutes or more before slicing.

Nutrition per slice
Calories 146, fat 4.4 g, carbs 23.6 g,
sodium 167 mg, protein 3.8 g

Cinnamon Rum Bread

Makes 1 loaf

Ingredients

<u>16 slice bread (2 pounds)</u>
1⅛ cups lukewarm water
1 egg, at room temperature
¼ cup butter, melted and cooled
¼ cup sugar
4 teaspoons rum extract
1⅔ teaspoons table salt
4 cups white bread flour
1⅓ teaspoons ground cinnamon
¼ teaspoon ground nutmeg
1⅓ teaspoons bread machine yeast

<u>12 slice bread (1½ pounds)</u>
¾ cup lukewarm water
1 egg, at room temperature
3 tablespoons butter, melted and cooled
3 tablespoons sugar
1 tablespoon rum extract
1¼ teaspoons table salt
3 cups white bread flour
1 teaspoon ground cinnamon
¼ teaspoon ground nutmeg
1 teaspoon bread machine yeast

Directions
1. Choose the size of loaf you would like to make and measure your ingredients.
2. Add the ingredients to the bread pan in the order listed above.

3. Place the pan in the bread machine and close the lid.
4. Turn on the bread maker. Select the Sweet setting, then the loaf size, and finally the crust color. Start the cycle.
5. When the cycle is finished and the bread is baked, carefully remove the pan from the machine. Use a pot holder as the handle will be very hot. Let rest for a few minutes.
6. Remove the bread from the pan and allow to cool on a wire rack for at least 10 minutes before slicing.

Nutrition per slice
Calories 156, fat 3.7 g, carbs 26.3 g,
sodium 248 mg, protein 4.3 g

Sweet Pineapple Bread

Makes 1 loaf

Ingredients

<u>16 slice bread (2 pounds)</u>
½ cup unsalted butter, melted
2 eggs, at room temperature
¾ cup coconut milk, at room temperature
¾ cup pineapple juice, at room temperature
1⅓ cups sugar
2 teaspoons coconut extract
3 cups all-purpose flour
1 cup shredded sweetened coconut
1⅓ teaspoons baking powder
¾ teaspoon table salt

<u>12 slice bread (1½ pounds)</u>
6 tablespoons unsalted butter, melted
2 eggs, at room temperature
½ cup coconut milk, at room temperature
½ cup pineapple juice, at room temperature
1 cup sugar
1½ teaspoons coconut extract
2 cups all-purpose flour
¾ cup shredded sweetened coconut
1 teaspoon baking powder
½ teaspoon table salt

Directions
1. Choose the size of loaf you would like to make and measure your ingredients.
2. Add the ingredients to the bread pan in the order listed above.

3. Place the pan in the bread machine and close the lid.
4. Turn on the bread maker. Select the Quick/Rapid setting, then the loaf size, and finally the crust color. Start the cycle.
5. When the cycle is finished and the bread is baked, carefully remove the pan from the machine. Use a pot holder as the handle will be very hot. Let rest for a few minutes.
6. Remove the bread from the pan and allow to cool on a wire rack for at least 10 minutes before slicing.

Nutrition per slice
Calories 139, fat 3.1 g, carbs 25.7 g,
sodium 238 mg, protein 4.2 g

Cocoa Banana Bread

Makes 1 loaf

Ingredients

<u>16 slice bread (2 pounds)</u>
4 bananas, mashed
3 eggs, at room temperature
1 cup packed light brown sugar
¾ cup unsalted butter, melted
¾ cup sour cream, at room temperature
⅓ cup sugar
2 teaspoons pure vanilla extract
1⅓ cups all-purpose flour
⅔ cup quick oats
3 tablespoons unsweetened cocoa powder
1⅓ teaspoons baking soda

<u>12 slice bread (1½ pounds)</u>
3 bananas, mashed
2 eggs, at room temperature
¾ cup packed light brown sugar
½ cup unsalted butter, melted
½ cup sour cream, at room temperature
¼ cup sugar
1½ teaspoons pure vanilla extract
1 cup all-purpose flour
½ cup quick oats
2 tablespoons unsweetened cocoa powder
1 teaspoon baking soda

Directions

1. Choose the size of loaf you would like to make and measure your ingredients.
2. Add the ingredients to the bread pan in the order listed above.
3. Place the pan in the bread machine and close the lid.
4. Turn on the bread maker. Select the Quick/Rapid setting, then the loaf size, and finally the crust color. Start the cycle.
5. When the cycle is finished and the bread is baked, carefully remove the pan from the machine. Use a pot holder as the handle will be very hot. Let rest for a few minutes.
6. Remove the bread from the pan and allow to cool on a wire rack for at least 10 minutes before slicing.

Nutrition per slice

Calories 223, fat 10.6 g, carbs 29.2 g,
sodium 163 mg, protein 4.5 g

Coconut Delight Bread

Makes 1 loaf

Ingredients

<u>16 slice bread (2 pounds)</u>
1⅓ cups lukewarm milk
1 egg, at room temperature
2 tablespoons unsalted butter, melted
2⅔ teaspoons pure coconut extract
3⅓ tablespoons sugar
1 teaspoon table salt
⅔ cup sweetened shredded coconut
4 cups white bread flour
2 teaspoons bread machine yeast

<u>12 slice bread (1½ pounds)</u>
1 cup lukewarm milk
1 egg, at room temperature
1½ tablespoons unsalted butter, melted
2 teaspoons pure coconut extract
2½ tablespoons sugar
¾ teaspoon table salt
½ cup sweetened shredded coconut
3 cups white bread flour
1½ teaspoons bread machine yeast

Directions
1. Choose the size of loaf you would like to make and measure your ingredients.
2. Add the ingredients to the bread pan in the order listed above.
3. Place the pan in the bread machine and close the lid.

4. Turn on the bread maker. Select the Sweet setting, then the loaf size, and finally the crust color. Start the cycle.
5. When the cycle is finished and the bread is baked, carefully remove the pan from the machine. Use a pot holder as the handle will be very hot. Let rest for a few minutes.
6. Remove the bread from the pan and allow to cool down on a wire rack for at least 10 minutes or more before slicing.

Nutrition per slice
Calories 168, fat 3.8 g, carbs 26.4 g,
sodium 163 mg, protein 5.1 g

Chocolate Chip Bread

Makes 1 loaf

Ingredients

<u>16 slice bread (2 pounds)</u>
1⅓ cups sour cream
3 eggs, at room temperature
1⅓ cups sugar
¾ cup unsalted butter, melted
⅓ cup plain Greek yogurt
2¼ cups all-purpose flour
⅔ cup unsweetened cocoa powder
⅔ teaspoon baking powder
⅔ teaspoon table salt
1⅓ cups milk chocolate chips

<u>12 slice bread (1½ pounds)</u>
1 cup sour cream
2 eggs, at room temperature
1 cup sugar
½ cup unsalted butter, melted
¼ cup plain Greek yogurt
1¾ cups all-purpose flour
½ cup unsweetened cocoa powder
½ teaspoon baking powder
½ teaspoon table salt
1 cup milk chocolate chips

Directions
1. Choose the size of loaf you would like to make and measure your ingredients.
2. Add the ingredients to the bread pan in the order listed above.

3. Place the pan in the bread machine and close the lid.
4. Turn on the bread maker. Select the Quick/Rapid setting, then the loaf size, and finally the crust color. Start the cycle.
5. When the cycle is finished and the bread is baked, carefully remove the pan from the machine. Use a pot holder as the handle will be very hot. Let rest for a few minutes.
6. Remove the bread from the pan and allow to cool down on a wire rack for at least 10 minutes or more before slicing.

Nutrition per slice
Calories 338, fat 15.4 g, carbs 36.8 g, sodium 243 mg, protein 6.2 g

Sweet Vanilla Bread

Makes 1 loaf

Ingredients

16 slice bread (2 pounds)
¾ cup lukewarm milk
¼ cup unsalted butter, melted
¼ cup sugar
1 egg, at room temperature
2 teaspoons pure vanilla extract
½ teaspoon almond extract
3⅓ cups white bread flour
2 teaspoons bread machine yeast

12 slice bread (1½ pounds)
½ cup + 1 tablespoon lukewarm milk
3 tablespoons unsalted butter, melted
3 tablespoons sugar
1 egg, at room temperature
1½ teaspoons pure vanilla extract
⅓ teaspoon almond extract
2½ cups white bread flour
1½ teaspoons bread machine yeast

Directions
1. Choose the size of loaf you would like to make and measure your ingredients.
2. Add the ingredients to the bread pan in the order listed above.
3. Place the pan in the bread machine and close the lid.
4. Turn on the bread maker. Select the White/Basic setting, then the loaf size, and finally the crust color. Start the cycle.

5. When the cycle is finished and the bread is baked, carefully remove the pan from the machine. Use a pot holder as the handle will be very hot. Let rest for a few minutes.
6. Remove the bread from the pan and allow to cool on a wire rack for at least 10 minutes before slicing.

Nutrition per slice
Calories 137, fat 4.2 g, carbs 23.4 g, sodium 46 mg, protein 4 g

SPECIALTY AND HOLIDAY BREADS

Challah Bread

Makes 1 loaf

Ingredients
<u>16 slice bread (2 pounds)</u>
1 cup +¾ teaspoon water, lukewarm between 80 and 90°F
2 ½ tablespoons unsalted butter, melted
2 small eggs, beaten
2 ½ tablespoons sugar
1 ¾ teaspoons salt
4 ½ cups white bread flour
2 teaspoons bread machine yeast or rapid rise yeast

<u>12 slice bread (1 ½ pounds)</u>
¾ cup +1 tablespoon water, lukewarm between 80 and 90°F
2 tablespoons unsalted butter, melted
1 egg, beaten
2 tablespoons sugar
1 ½ teaspoons salt
3 ¼ cups white bread flour
1 ½ teaspoons bread machine yeast or rapid rise yeast

<u>For oven baking</u>
1 egg yolk
2 tablespoons cold water
1 tablespoon poppy seed (optional)

Directions
1. Choose the size of loaf you would like to make and measure your ingredients.
2. Add the ingredients to the bread pan in the order listed above.
3. Place the pan in the bread machine and close the lid.
4. Turn on the bread maker. Select the Dough setting, then the loaf size, and finally the crust color. Start the cycle.
5. Lightly flour a working surface and prepare a large baking sheet by greasing it with cooking spray or vegetable oil or line with parchment paper or a silicone mat.
6. Pre-heat the oven to 375°F and place oven rack in the middle position.
7. After the dough cycle is done, carefully remove the dough from the pan and place it on the working surface. Divide dough in three even parts.
8. Roll each part into 13-inch-long cables for the 1 ½ pound Challah bread or 17-inch for the 2-pound loaf. Arrange the dough cables side by side and start braiding from its middle part.
9. In order to make a seal, pinch ends and tuck the ends under braid.
10. Arrange the loaf onto the baking sheet; cover the sheet with a clean kitchen towel. Let rise for 45-60 minutes or more until it doubles in size.
11. In a mixing bowl, mix the egg yolk and cold water to make an egg wash. Gently brush the egg wash over the loaf. Sprinkle top with the poppy seed, if desired.
12. Bake for about 25-30 minutes or until loaf turns golden brown and is fully cooked.

Nutrition per slice
Calories 196, fat 3.3g, carbs 33.5 g, sodium 207, protein 6.4g

Dry Fruit Cinnamon Bread

Makes 1 loaf

Ingredients

<u>16 slice bread (2 pounds)</u>
1⅔ cups lukewarm milk
⅓ cup unsalted butter, melted
⅔ teaspoon pure vanilla extract
¼ teaspoon pure almond extract
⅓ cup light brown sugar
1⅓ teaspoons table salt
2 teaspoons ground cinnamon
4 cups white bread flour
1⅔ teaspoons bread machine yeast
⅔ cup dried mixed fruit
⅔ cup golden raisins, chopped

<u>12 slice bread (1½ pounds)</u>
1¼ cups lukewarm milk
¼ cup unsalted butter, melted
½ teaspoon pure vanilla extract
¼ teaspoon pure almond extract
3 tablespoons light brown sugar
1 teaspoon table salt
2 teaspoons ground cinnamon
3 cups white bread flour
1 teaspoon bread machine yeast
½ cup dried mixed fruit
½ cup golden raisins, chopped

Directions

1. Choose the size of loaf you would like to make and measure your ingredients.
2. Add all of the ingredients except for the mixed fruit and raisins to the bread pan in the order listed above.
3. Place the pan in the bread machine and close the lid.
4. Turn on the bread maker. Select the White/Basic or Fruit/Nut (if your machine has this setting) setting, then the loaf size, and finally the crust color. Start the cycle.
5. When the machine signals to add ingredients, add the mixed fruit and raisins. (Some machines have a fruit/nut hopper where you can add the mixed fruit and raisins when you start the machine. The machine will automatically add them to the dough during the baking process.)
6. When the cycle is finished and the bread is baked, carefully remove the pan from the machine. Use a pot holder as the handle will be very hot. Let rest for a few minutes.
7. Remove the bread from the pan and allow to cool on a wire rack for at least 10 minutes before slicing.

Nutrition per slice
Calories 193, fat 4.7 g, carbs 29.3 g, sodium 226 mg, protein 5 g

Beer Pizza Dough

Makes 1 dough

Ingredients

<u>16 pizza slices (2 pounds)</u>
1⅓ cups beer, at room temperature
¼ cup olive oil
1⅓ tablespoons sugar
1⅓ teaspoons table salt
4 cups white bread flour or all-purpose flour
2 teaspoons bread machine yeast

<u>12 pizza slices (1½ pounds)</u>
1 cup beer, at room temperature
3 tablespoons olive oil
1 tablespoon sugar
1 teaspoon table salt
3 cups white bread flour or all-purpose flour
1½ teaspoons bread machine yeast

Directions

1. Choose the size of dough you would like to make and measure your ingredients.
2. Add the ingredients to the bread pan in the order listed above.
3. Place the pan in the bread machine and close the lid.
4. Turn on the bread maker. Select the Dough setting and then the dough size. Start the machine.
5. When the cycle is finished, carefully remove the dough from the pan.
6. Place the dough on a lightly floured surface and roll to make a pizza crust of your desired thickness. Set aside for 10–15 minutes.

7. Top with your favorite pizza sauce, toppings, cheese, etc.
8. Bake in an oven at 400°F or 204°C for 15–20 minutes or until the edges turn light golden.

Nutrition per slice
Calories 121, fat 3.1 g, carbs 21.2 g, sodium 146 mg, protein 3 g

Basil Pizza Dough

Makes 1 dough

Ingredients

<u>16 pizza slices (2 pounds)</u>
1¼ cups lukewarm water
¼ cup olive oil
1¼ teaspoons table salt
2 teaspoons sugar
2 teaspoons basil, dried
4 cups white bread flour or all-purpose flour
2 teaspoons bread machine yeast

<u>12 pizza slices (1½ pounds)</u>
1 cup lukewarm water
3 tablespoons olive oil
1 teaspoon table salt
1½ teaspoons sugar
1½ teaspoons basil, dried
3 cups white bread flour or all-purpose flour
1½ teaspoons bread machine yeast

Directions

1. Choose the size of dough you would like to make and measure your ingredients.
2. Add the ingredients to the bread pan in the order listed above.
3. Place the pan in the bread machine and close the lid.
4. Turn on the bread maker. Select the Dough setting and then the dough size. Start the machine.
5. When the cycle is finished, carefully remove the dough from the pan.

6. Place the dough on a lightly floured surface and roll to make a pizza crust of your desired thickness. Set aside for 10–15 minutes.
7. Top with your favorite pizza sauce, toppings, cheese, etc.
8. Bake in an oven at 400°F or 204°C for 15–20 minutes or until the edges turn light golden.

Nutrition per slice
Calories 146, fat 3.6 g, carbs 23.4 g, sodium 157 mg, protein 4 g

Classic Sourdough Bread

Makes 1 loaf

Ingredients
Sourdough Starter
2 cups lukewarm water
2 cups all-purpose flour
2½ teaspoons bread machine yeast

16 slice bread (2 pounds)
2⅔ tablespoons lukewarm water
2⅔ cups sourdough starter
2⅔ tablespoons unsalted butter, melted
2⅔ teaspoons sugar
2 teaspoons salt
3⅓ cups white bread flour
2 teaspoons bread machine yeast

12 slice bread (1½ pounds)
2 tablespoons lukewarm water
2 cups sourdough starter
2 tablespoons unsalted butter, melted
2 teaspoons sugar
1½ teaspoons salt
2½ cups white bread flour
1½ teaspoons bread machine yeast

Directions
Starter:
1. Add the water, flour and yeast to a medium-size non-metallic bowl. Mix well until no lumps are visible.

2. Cover the bowl loosely and leave it in a warm area of your kitchen for 5–8 days. Do not place in a fridge or under direct sunlight.
3. Stir the mixture several times every day. Always put the cover back on the bowl afterwards.
4. The starter is ready to use when it appears bubbly and has a sour smell.

Sourdough Bread:
1. Choose the size of loaf you would like to make and measure your ingredients.
2. Add the ingredients to the bread pan in the order listed above.
3. Place the pan in the bread machine and close the lid.
4. Turn on the bread maker. Select the White/Basic setting, then the loaf size, and finally the crust color. Start the cycle.
5. When the cycle is finished and the bread is baked, carefully remove the pan from the machine. Use a pot holder as the handle will be very hot. Let rest for a few minutes.
6. Remove the bread from the pan and allow to cool on a wire rack for at least 10 minutes before slicing.

Nutrition per slice
Calories 158, fat 2.3 g, carbs 28 g, sodium 311 mg, protein 4.5 g

Milk Honey Sourdough Bread

Makes 1 loaf

Ingredients

<u>16 slice bread (2 pounds)</u>
½ cup lukewarm milk
2 cups sourdough starter
¼ cup olive oil
2 tablespoons honey
1⅓ teaspoons salt
4 cups white bread flour
1⅓ teaspoons bread machine yeast

<u>12 slice bread (1½ pounds)</u>
⅓ cup lukewarm milk
1½ cups sourdough starter
3 tablespoons olive oil
1½ tablespoons honey
1 teaspoon salt
3 cups white bread flour
1 teaspoon bread machine yeast

Directions
1. Choose the size of loaf you would like to make and measure your ingredients.
2. Add the ingredients to the bread pan in the order listed above.
3. Place the pan in the bread machine and close the lid.
4. Turn on the bread maker. Select the White/Basic setting, then the loaf size, and finally the crust color. Start the cycle.

5. When the cycle is finished and the bread is baked, carefully remove the pan from the machine. Use a pot holder as the handle will be very hot. Let rest for a few minutes.
6. Remove the bread from the pan and allow to cool on a wire rack for at least 10 minutes before slicing.

Nutrition per slice
Calories 186, fat 3.7 g, carbs 32.2 g, sodium 207 mg, protein 4 g

Cherry Christmas Bread

Makes 1 loaf

Ingredients

<u>16 slice bread (2 pounds)</u>
1 cup + 1 tablespoon lukewarm milk
1 egg, at room temperature
2 tablespoons unsalted butter, melted
3 tablespoons light brown sugar
⅛ teaspoon ground cinnamon
4 cups white bread flour, divided
1½ teaspoons bread machine yeast
⅔ cup candied cherries
½ cup chopped almonds
½ cup raisins, chopped

<u>12 slice bread (1½ pounds)</u>
¾ cup lukewarm milk
1 egg, at room temperature
1½ tablespoons unsalted butter, melted
2¼ tablespoons light brown sugar
⅛ teaspoon ground cinnamon
3 cups white bread flour, divided
1⅛ teaspoons bread machine yeast
½ cup candied cherries
⅓ cup chopped almonds
⅓ cup raisins, chopped

Directions
1. Choose the size of loaf you would like to make and measure your ingredients.
2. Add all of the ingredients except for the cherries, raisins and almonds to the bread pan in the order listed above.

3. Place the pan in the bread machine and close the lid.
4. Turn on the bread maker. Select the White/Basic or Fruit/Nut (if your machine has this setting) setting, then the loaf size, and finally the crust color. Start the cycle.
5. When the machine signals to add ingredients, add the cherries, raisins and almonds. (Some machines have a fruit/nut hopper where you can add the cherries, raisins and almonds when you start the machine. The machine will automatically add them to the dough during the baking process.)
6. When the cycle is finished and the bread is baked, carefully remove the pan from the machine. Use a pot holder as the handle will be very hot. Let rest for a few minutes.
7. Remove the bread from the pan and allow to cool on a wire rack for at least 10 minutes before slicing.

Nutrition per slice
Calories 176, fat 4.2 g, carbs 32.7 g, sodium 46 mg, protein 5.1 g

Coffee Caraway Seed Bread

Makes 1 loaf

Ingredients

16 slice bread (2 pounds)
1 cup lukewarm water
½ cup brewed coffee, lukewarm
2 tablespoons balsamic vinegar
2 tablespoons olive oil
2 tablespoons dark molasses
1 tablespoon light brown sugar
1 teaspoon table salt
2 teaspoons caraway seeds
¼ cup unsweetened cocoa powder
1 cup dark rye flour
2½ cups white bread flour
2 teaspoons bread machine yeast

12 slice bread (1½ pounds)
¾ cup lukewarm water
⅓ cup brewed coffee, lukewarm
1½ tablespoons balsamic vinegar
1½ tablespoons olive oil
1½ tablespoons dark molasses
¾ tablespoon light brown sugar
¾ teaspoon table salt
1½ teaspoons caraway seeds
3 tablespoons unsweetened cocoa powder
¾ cup dark rye flour
1¾ cups white bread flour
1½ teaspoons bread machine yeast

Directions
1. Choose the size of loaf you would like to make and measure your ingredients.
2. Add the ingredients to the bread pan in the order listed above.
3. Place the pan in the bread machine and close the lid.
4. Turn on the bread maker. Select the Whole Wheat/Wholegrain setting, then the loaf size, and finally the crust color. Start the cycle.
5. When the cycle is finished and the bread is baked, carefully remove the pan from the machine. Use a pot holder as the handle will be very hot. Let rest for a few minutes.
6. Remove the bread from the pan and allow to cool down on a wire rack for at least 10 minutes or more before slicing.

Nutrition per slice
Calories 126, fat 1.8 g, carbs 22.6 g, sodium 148 mg, protein 4 g

Cinnamon Beer Bread

Makes 1 loaf

Ingredients

<u>16 slice bread (2 pounds)</u>
2 cups beer, at room temperature
1 cup unsalted butter, melted
⅓ cup honey
4 cups all-purpose flour
1⅓ teaspoons table salt
⅓ teaspoon ground cinnamon
1⅓ tablespoons baking powder

<u>12 slice bread (1½ pounds)</u>
1½ cups beer, at room temperature
⅓ cup unsalted butter, melted
¼ cup honey
3 cups all-purpose flour
1 teaspoon table salt
¼ teaspoon ground cinnamon
1 tablespoon baking powder

Directions
1. Choose the size of loaf you would like to make and measure your ingredients.
2. Add the ingredients to the bread pan in the order listed above.
3. Place the pan in the bread machine and close the lid.
4. Turn on the bread maker. Select the Quick/Rapid setting, then the loaf size, and finally the crust color. Start the cycle.

5. When the cycle is finished and the bread is baked, carefully remove the pan from the machine. Use a pot holder as the handle will be very hot. Let rest for a few minutes.
6. Remove the bread from the pan and allow to cool on a wire rack for at least 10 minutes before slicing.

Nutrition per slice
Calories 186, fat 4.6 g, carbs 26.4 g,
sodium 217 mg, protein 3.5 g

French Butter Bread

Makes 1 loaf

Ingredients

<u>16 slice bread (2 pounds)</u>
¾ cup lukewarm milk
4 eggs, at room temperature
2⅔ tablespoons sugar
1 teaspoon table salt
½ cup + 3⅓ tablespoons unsalted butter, melted
4 cups white bread flour
2 teaspoons bread machine yeast

<u>12 slice bread (1½ pounds)</u>
½ cup + 1 tablespoon lukewarm milk
3 eggs, at room temperature
2 tablespoons sugar
¾ teaspoon table salt
½ cup unsalted butter, melted
3 cups white bread flour
1½ teaspoons bread machine yeast

Directions

1. Choose the size of loaf you would like to make and measure your ingredients.
2. Add the ingredients to the bread pan in the order listed above.
3. Place the pan in the bread machine and close the lid.
4. Turn on the bread maker. Select the White/Basic setting, then the loaf size, and finally the crust color. Start the cycle.

5. When the cycle is finished and the bread is baked, carefully remove the pan from the machine. Use a pot holder as the handle will be very hot. Let rest for a few minutes.
6. Remove the bread from the pan and allow to cool on a wire rack for at least 10 minutes before slicing.

Nutrition per slice
Calories 208, fat 8.8 g, carbs 24.3 g, sodium 221 mg, protein 5.8 g

Holiday Chocolate Bread

Makes 1 loaf

Ingredients

<u>16 slice bread (2 pounds)</u>
1 cup + 3 tablespoons lukewarm milk
1 egg, at room temperature
2 tablespoons unsalted butter, melted
1½ teaspoons pure vanilla extract
2⅔ tablespoons sugar
1 teaspoon table salt
4 cups white bread flour
1⅓ teaspoons bread machine yeast
⅔ cup white chocolate chips
½ cup dried cranberries

<u>12 slice bread (1½ pounds)</u>
⅞ cup lukewarm milk
1 egg, at room temperature
1½ tablespoons unsalted butter, melted
1 teaspoon pure vanilla extract
2 tablespoons sugar
¾ teaspoon table salt
3 cups white bread flour
1 teaspoon bread machine yeast
½ cup white chocolate chips
⅓ cup dried cranberries

Directions
1. Choose the size of loaf you would like to make and measure your ingredients.
2. Add all of the ingredients except for the chocolate chips and cranberries to the bread pan in the order listed above.

3. Place the pan in the bread machine and close the lid.
4. Turn on the bread maker. Select the White/Basic or Fruit/Nut (if your machine has this setting) setting, then the loaf size, and finally the crust color. Start the cycle.
5. When the machine signals to add ingredients, add the chocolate chips and cranberries. (Some machines have a fruit/nut hopper where you can add the chocolate chips and cranberries when you start the machine. The machine will automatically add them to the dough during the baking process.)
6. When the cycle is finished and the bread is baked, carefully remove the pan from the machine. Use a pot holder as the handle will be very hot. Let rest for a few minutes.
7. Remove the bread from the pan and allow to cool on a wire rack for at least 10 minutes before slicing.

Nutrition per slice
Calories 204, fat 4.6 g, carbs 31.7 g,
sodium 164 mg, protein 4.5 g

New Year Spiced Bread

Makes 1 loaf

Ingredients

<u>16 slice bread (2 pounds)</u>
½ cup brewed coffee, cooled to room temperature
⅔ cup unsalted butter, melted
⅔ cup honey
1 cup sugar
⅓ cup dark brown sugar
2 eggs, at room temperature
3 tablespoons whiskey
⅓ cup orange juice, at room temperature
1⅓ teaspoons pure vanilla extract
3 cups all-purpose flour
⅔ tablespoon ground cinnamon
⅔ teaspoon baking soda
⅓ teaspoon ground allspice
⅓ teaspoon table salt
⅓ teaspoon ground cloves
⅔ tablespoon baking powder

<u>12 slice bread (1½ pounds)</u>
⅓ cup brewed coffee, cooled to room temperature
½ cup unsalted butter, melted
½ cup honey
¾ cup sugar
¼ cup dark brown sugar
2 eggs, at room temperature
2 tablespoons whiskey
¼ cup orange juice, at room temperature
1 teaspoon pure vanilla extract
2 cups all-purpose flour

½ tablespoon ground cinnamon
½ teaspoon baking soda
¼ teaspoon ground allspice
¼ teaspoon table salt
¼ teaspoon ground cloves
½ tablespoon baking powder

Directions

1. Choose the size of loaf you would like to make and measure your ingredients.
2. Add the ingredients to the bread pan in the order listed above.
3. Place the pan in the bread machine and close the lid.
4. Turn on the bread maker. Select the Quick/Rapid setting, then the loaf size, and finally the crust color. Start the cycle.
5. When the cycle is finished and the bread is baked, carefully remove the pan from the machine. Use a pot holder as the handle will be very hot. Let rest for a few minutes.
6. Remove the bread from the pan and allow to cool on a wire rack for at least 10 minutes before slicing.

Nutrition per slice

Calories 271, fat 8.7 g, carbs 38.3 g,
sodium 168 mg, protein 3.4 g

Cocoa Holiday Bread

Makes 1 loaf

Ingredients

<u>16 slice bread (2 pounds)</u>
1 cup brewed coffee, lukewarm
½ cup evaporated milk, lukewarm
2 tablespoons unsalted butter, melted
3 tablespoons honey
1 tablespoon dark molasses
1 tablespoon sugar
4 teaspoons unsweetened cocoa powder
1 teaspoon table salt
2¼ cups whole-wheat bread flour
2¼ cups white bread flour
2¼ teaspoons bread machine yeast

<u>12 slice bread (1½ pounds)</u>
¾ cup brewed coffee, lukewarm
⅓ cup evaporated milk, lukewarm
1½ tablespoons unsalted butter, melted
2¼ tablespoons honey
¾ tablespoon dark molasses
¾ tablespoon sugar
1 tablespoon unsweetened cocoa powder
¾ teaspoon table salt
1⅔ cups whole-wheat bread flour
1⅔ cups white bread flour
1⅔ teaspoons bread machine yeast

Directions
1. Choose the size of loaf you would like to make and measure your ingredients.
2. Add the ingredients to the bread pan in the order listed above.
3. Place the pan in the bread machine and close the lid.
4. Turn on the bread maker. Select the Sweet setting, then the loaf size, and finally the crust color. Start the cycle.
5. When the cycle is finished and the bread is baked, carefully remove the pan from the machine. Use a pot holder as the handle will be very hot. Let rest for a few minutes.
6. Remove the bread from the pan and allow to cool on a wire rack for at least 10 minutes before slicing.

Nutrition per slice
Calories 173, fat 2.3 g, carbs 32.4 g, sodium 156 mg, protein 4.4 g

Holiday Eggnog Bread

Makes 1 loaf

Ingredients

16 slice bread (2 pounds)
1½ cups eggnog, at room temperature
1½ tablespoons unsalted butter, melted
2 tablespoons sugar
1¼ teaspoons table salt
½ teaspoon ground cinnamon
½ teaspoon ground nutmeg
4 cups white bread flour
1¾ teaspoons bread machine yeast

12 slice bread (1½ pounds)
1⅛ cups eggnog, at room temperature
1⅛ tablespoons unsalted butter, melted
1½ tablespoons sugar
1 teaspoon table salt
⅓ teaspoon ground cinnamon
⅓ teaspoon ground nutmeg
3 cups white bread flour
1⅓ teaspoons bread machine yeast

Directions

1. Choose the size of loaf you would like to make and measure your ingredients.
2. Add the ingredients to the bread pan in the order listed above.
3. Place the pan in the bread machine and close the lid.
4. Turn on the bread maker. Select the White/Basic setting, then the loaf size, and finally the crust color. Start the cycle.

5. When the cycle is finished and the bread is baked, carefully remove the pan from the machine. Use a pot holder as the handle will be very hot. Let rest for a few minutes.
6. Remove the bread from the pan and allow to cool on a wire rack for at least 10 minutes before slicing.

Nutrition per slice
Calories 167, fat 2.8 g, carbs 28.6 g,
sodium 219 mg, protein 3.8 g

Easter Bread

Makes 1 loaf

Ingredients

<u>16 slice bread (2 pounds)</u>
1 cup lukewarm milk
2 eggs, at room temperature
2⅔ tablespoons unsalted butter, melted
⅓ cup sugar
1 teaspoon table salt
2⅓ teaspoons lemon zest
4 cups white bread flour
2¼ teaspoons bread machine yeast

<u>12 slice bread (1½ pounds)</u>
¾ cup lukewarm milk
2 eggs, at room temperature
2 tablespoons unsalted butter, melted
¼ cup sugar
1 teaspoon table salt
2 teaspoons lemon zest
3 cups white bread flour
2 teaspoons bread machine yeast

Directions

1. Choose the size of loaf you would like to make and measure your ingredients.
2. Add the ingredients to the bread pan in the order listed above.
3. Place the pan in the bread machine and close the lid.
4. Turn on the bread maker. Select the White/Basic setting, then the loaf size, and finally the crust color. Start the cycle.

5. When the cycle is finished and the bread is baked, carefully remove the pan from the machine. Use a pot holder as the handle will be very hot. Let rest for a few minutes.
6. Remove the bread from the pan and allow to cool on a wire rack for at least 10 minutes before slicing.

Nutrition per slice
Calories 163, fat 3.4 g, carbs 27.3 g, sodium 217 mg, protein 4.4 g

RECIPE INDEX

Everyday & Multigrain Breads _____ 19
   Classic White Bread I _____ 19
   Classic White Bread II _____ 21
   Classic White Sandwich Bread _____ 23
   Baguette Style French Bread _____ 25
   100% Whole Wheat Bread _____ 27
   Buttermilk Bread _____ 29
   Oat Molasses Bread _____ 31
   Whole Wheat Corn Bread _____ 33
   Wheat Bran Bread _____ 35
   Rye Bread _____ 37
   Classic Whole Wheat Bread _____ 39
   Oat Bran Nutmeg Bread _____ 41
   Multigrain Honey Bread _____ 43
   Pumpernickel Bread _____ 45
   Classic Dark Bread _____ 47
   Classic Corn Bread _____ 49
   Basic Seed Bread _____ 51
   Basic Bulgur Bread _____ 53
   Oat Quinoa Bread _____ 55
   Whole Wheat Sunflower Bread _____ 57
   Honey Sunflower Bread _____ 59
   Flaxseed Milk Bread _____ 61
   Honey Wheat Bread _____ 63
   French Crusty Loaf Bread _____ 65
Gluten Free Breads _____ 67
   Classic White Bread _____ 67
   Pecan Apple Spice Bread _____ 69
   Pumpkin Jalapeno Bread _____ 71
   Walnut Banana Bread _____ 73
   Basic Honey Bread _____ 75
   Onion Buttermilk Bread _____ 77

Pecan Cranberry Bread ___ 79
Cheese Potato Bread ___ 81
Instant Cocoa Bread ___ 83
Mix Seed Bread ___ 85
Garlic Parsley Bread ___ 87
Italian Herb Bread ___ 89
Fruit Breads ___ 91
   Cinnamon Apple Bread ___ 91
   Blueberry Honey Bread ___ 93
   Raisin Candied Fruit Bread ___ 95
   Spice Peach Bread ___ 97
   Cocoa Date Bread ___ 99
   Strawberry Oat Bread ___ 101
   Cinnamon Figs Bread ___ 103
   Cranberry Honey Bread ___ 105
   Orange Bread ___ 107
   Honey Banana Bread ___ 109
   Garlic Olive Bread ___ 111
   Cinnamon Pumpkin Bread ___ 113
Spice and Nut Breads ___ 115
   Super Spice Bread ___ 115
   Almond Milk Bread ___ 117
   Cinnamon Milk Bread ___ 119
   Hazelnut Honey Bread ___ 121
   Cardamom Honey Bread ___ 123
   Pistachio Cherry Bread ___ 125
   Mix Seed Raisin Bread ___ 127
   Anise Honey Bread ___ 129
   Basic Pecan Bread ___ 131
Vegetable Breads ___ 133
   Beetroot Bread ___ 133
   Sweet Potato Bread ___ 135
   Basil Tomato Bread ___ 137
   Zucchini Spice Bread ___ 139
   Potato Honey Bread ___ 141

Onion Chive Bread _____ 143
Honey Potato Flakes Bread _____ 145
Zucchini Lemon Bread _____ 147
Cheese and Herb Breads _____ 149
   Romano Oregano Bread _____ 149
   Mexican Style Jalapeno Cheese Bread _____ 151
   Jalapeno Cheddar Bread _____ 153
   Parsley Garlic Bread _____ 155
   Cheddar Bacon Bread _____ 157
   Mixed Herb Cheese Bread _____ 159
   Basil Cheese Bread _____ 161
   American Cheese Beer Bread _____ 163
   Swiss Olive Bread _____ 165
   Parmesan Cheddar Bread _____ 167
   Honey Goat Cheese Bread _____ 169
Sweet Breads _____ 171
   Apple Honey Bread _____ 171
   White Chocolate Bread _____ 173
   Ginger Spiced Bread _____ 175
   Sweet Applesauce Bread _____ 177
   Milk Sweet Bread _____ 179
   Allspice Currant Bread _____ 181
   Buttermilk Pecan Bread _____ 183
   Cashew Butter/Peanut Butter Bread _____ 185
   Delicious Sour Cream Bread _____ 187
   Cinnamon Rum Bread _____ 189
   Sweet Pineapple Bread _____ 191
   Cocoa Banana Bread _____ 193
   Coconut Delight Bread _____ 195
   Chocolate Chip Bread _____ 197
   Sweet Vanilla Bread _____ 199
Specialty and Holiday Breads _____ 201
   Challah Bread _____ 201
   Dry Fruit Cinnamon Bread _____ 203
   Beer Pizza Dough _____ 205

Basil Pizza Dough	207
Classic Sourdough Bread	209
Milk Honey Sourdough Bread	211
Cherry Christmas Bread	213
Coffee Caraway Seed Bread	215
Cinnamon Beer Bread	217
French Butter Bread	219
Holiday Chocolate Bread	221
New Year Spiced Bread	223
Cocoa Holiday Bread	225
Holiday Eggnog Bread	227
Easter Bread	229

ALSO BY LOUISE DAVIDSON

SLOW COOKER
SOUP
Cookbook
Easy Crock Pot Soup Meal Recipes
Louise Davidson

FIX, COOK & SERVE
LOW CARB
SLOW COOKER
One-Pot Meals
Convenient 8-Hour +
Crock Pot Recipes
LOUISE DAVIDSON

Fix, Cook, & Serve!
Slow Cooker
COOKBOOK
Easy One-Pot Meal
Crock Pot Recipes
LOUISE DAVIDSON

Freezer Meals
Recipes
EASY ONE-POT MAKE AHEAD
DUMP MEALS
LOUISE DAVIDSON

CROCK POT
EXPRESS
COOKBOOK
Best Quick & Easy
Crock Pot Express
Multi Cooker Recipes
LOUISE DAVIDSON

CASSEROLES
FROM OVEN TO TABLE
EASY EVERYDAY CASSEROLE RECIPES
LOUISE DAVIDSON

CONVERSION TABLES

Measuring Equivalent Chart

3 teaspoons	1 tablespoon
2 tablespoons	1 ounce
4 tablespoons	¼ cup
8 tablespoons	½ cup
16 tablespoons	1 cup
2 cups	1 pint
4 cups	1 quart
4 quarts	1 gallon

Type	Imperial	Imperial	Metric
Weight	1 dry ounce		28g
	1 pound	16 dry ounces	0.45 kg
Volume	1 teaspoon		5 ml
	1 dessert spoon	2 teaspoons	10 ml
	1 tablespoon	3 teaspoons	15 ml
	1 Australian tablespoon	4 teaspoons	20 ml
	1 fluid ounce	2 tablespoons	30 ml
	1 cup	16 tablespoons	240 ml
	1 cup	8 fluid ounces	240 ml
	1 pint	2 cups	470 ml
	1 quart	2 pints	0.95 l
	1 gallon	4 quarts	3.8 l
Length	1 inch		2.54 cm

* Numbers are rounded to the closest equivalent

Gluten Free – Conversion Tables

All-Purpose Flour	Rice Flour	Potato Starch	Tapioca	Xanthan Gum
½ cup	1/3 cup	2 tablespoons	1 tablespoon	¼ teaspoon
1 cup	½ cup	3 tablespoons	1 tablespoon	½ teaspoon
¼ cup	¾ cup	1/3 cup	3 tablespoons	2/3 teaspoon
1 ½ cup	1 cup	5 tablespoons	3 tablespoons	2/3 teaspoon
1 ¾ cup	1 ¼ cup	5 tablespoons	3 tablespoons	1 teaspoon
2 cups	1 ½ cup	1/3 cup	1/3 cup	1 teaspoon
2 ½ cups	1 ½ cup	½ cup	¼ cup	1 1/8 teaspoon
2 2/3 cups	2 cups	½ cup	¼ cup	1 ¼ teaspoon
3 cups	2 cups	2/3 cup	1/3 cup	1 ½ cup

Flour: quantity and weight

Flour Amount
1 cup = 140 grams
3/4 cup = 105 grams
1/2 cup = 70 grams
1/4 cup = 35 grams

Sugar: quantity and weight

Sugar
1 cup = 200 grams
3/4 cup = 150 grams
2/3 cup = 135 grams
1/2 cup = 100 grams
1/3 cup = 70 grams
1/4 cup = 50 grams

Powdered Sugar
1 cup = 160 grams
3/4 cup = 120 grams
1/2 cup = 80 grams
1/4 cup = 40 grams

Cream: quantity and weight

Cream Amount
1 cup = 250 ml = 235 grams
3/4 cup = 188 ml = 175 grams
1/2 cup = 125 ml = 115 grams
1/4 cup = 63 ml = 60 grams
1 tablespoon = 15 ml = 15 grams

Butter: quantity and weight

Butter Amount
1 cup = 8 ounces = 2 sticks = 16 tablespoons = 230 grams
1/2 cup = 4 ounces = 1 stick = 8 tablespoons = 115 grams
¼ cup = 2 ounces = ½ stick = 4 tablespoons = 58 grams

Oven Temperature Equivalent Chart

Fahrenheit (°F)	Celsius (°C)	Gas Mark
220	100	
225	110	1/4
250	120	1/2
275	140	1
300	150	2
325	160	3
350	180	4
375	190	5
400	200	6
425	220	7
450	230	8
475	250	9
500	260	

* Celsius (°C) = T (°F)-32] * 5/9
** Fahrenheit (°F) = T (°C) * 9/5 + 32
*** Numbers are rounded to the closest equivalent

Printed in Great Britain
by Amazon